WISDOM'S FEAST

WISDOM'S FEAST

An Invitation to Feminist Interpretation of the Scriptures

Barbara E. Reid, O.P.

WILLIAM B. EERDMANS PUBLISHING COMPANY
GRAND RAPIDS, MICHIGAN

Wm. B. Eerdmans Publishing Co.
2140 Oak Industrial Drive N.E., Grand Rapids, Michigan 49505
www.eerdmans.com

ISBN 978-0-8028-7351-4

Library of Congress Cataloging-in-Publication Data

Names: Reid, Barbara E., author.
Title: Wisdom's feast : an invitation to feminist interpretation of the scriptures /
    Barbara E. Reid, O.P.
Description: Grand Rapids : Eerdmans Publishing Company, 2016. |
    Includes bibliographical references.
Identifiers: LCCN 2016013134 | ISBN 9780802873514 (pbk. : alk. paper)
Subjects: LCSH: Bible—Feminist criticism. | Bible and feminism.
Classification: LCC BS521.4 .R45 2016 | DDC 220.6082—dc23
    LC record available at https://lccn.loc.gov/2016013134

In loving memory of Christine F. Reid,

whose table was always bountiful and inclusive of all

Contents

Acknowledgments

It is with deep gratitude that I thank all those who have helped to shape my feminist consciousness and who have taught me ways of feminist biblical interpretation: my mother, Christine F. Reid, whose keen sense of equal dignity for all remains ever a part of me; my first teachers and now my companions in life and mission, the Dominican Sisters of Adrian and Grand Rapids, Michigan; my professors at the Catholic University of America, especially Elizabeth Johnson and Mary Ann Getty Sullivan; my colleagues, students, and staff at Catholic Theological Union, who continue to stretch and support me; and countless scholars and friends whose insights and wisdom constantly open new horizons for me.

Abbreviations

Ant.	Josephus, *Jewish Antiquities*
BAR	*Biblical Archaeology Review*
BDAG	*A Greek-English Lexicon of the New Testament and Other Early Christian Literature.* 3d ed. Revised and edited by Frederick William Danker. Chicago: University of Chicago Press, 2000
BJS	Brown Judaic Studies
BTB	*Biblical Theology Bulletin*
CBQ	*Catholic Biblical Quarterly*
CCEL	Christian Classics Ethereal Library
CNT	Companions to the New Testament
DRev	*Downside Review*
FCNT	Feminist Companion to the New Testament and Early Christian Writings
GNS	Good News Studies
ICC	International Critical Commentary
IFT	Introductions in Feminist Theology
Int	*Interpretation*
JBL	*Journal of Biblical Literature*
J.W.	Josephus, *Jewish War*
KJV	King James Version
NAB	New American Bible
NASB	New American Standard Bible
NEB	New English Bible
NJB	New Jerusalem Bible
NRSV	New Revised Standard Version
NTR	*New Theology Review*

Abbreviations

OBT	Overtures to Biblical Theology
OECS	Oxford Early Christian Studies
PG	Migne, *Patrologia Graeca*
PTMS	Princeton Theological Monograph Series
SBLSymS	Society of Biblical Literature Symposium Series
SVC	Supplements to Vigiliae Christianae

Introduction

"Come, eat of my bread and drink of the wine I have mixed. Lay aside immaturity and live and walk in the way of insight." This is the invitation of Woman Wisdom in the book of Proverbs (9:5-6) to any who want to learn her wise ways.[1] Eating at her "banquet" is the image for the rich and satisfying teaching that she offers, meant to help all who partake of it to live wisely and well. This book has a similar aim. It seeks to provide a smorgasbord of tantalizing new interpretations of familiar texts from the Scriptures—interpretations that rely on women's wisdom and that draw from the biblical texts a way of life that promotes equal dignity and value for all, women and men alike.

Just as Wisdom offered her banquet to those who were "simple," so too this book is intended for Christians who do not have scholarly training in biblical studies but who are hungry to learn from the rich insights of feminist biblical scholars. Questions at the end of each chapter can be used either for personal reflection or for discussion with groups devoted to Bible study.

Forerunners in Feminist Biblical Interpretation

It is nothing new for women to interpret the Bible through the lenses of their own experience. In every age, women have turned to the Scriptures to encounter God, to help make meaning of their lives, and to find guidance

---

1. Unless otherwise indicated, all Scripture quotations are taken from the New Revised Standard Version (NRSV).

for themselves, their families, and their communities on how to live life well in God's embrace. Even women who cannot read learn and recite the stories orally. Because women in the past did not have as much access to formal theological education as did men, very little of women's reflections on the Bible has been preserved. Only in recent decades have women made gains in formal academic and church settings, becoming biblical scholars, teachers, preachers, and pastors, where they have begun to develop their own methods of biblical interpretation.

One of the outstanding forerunners in this endeavor was Elizabeth Cady Stanton, an American suffragist who lived from 1815 to 1902. She noted that, whenever women tried to make inroads into politics, education, or the work world, the Bible was quoted to argue that such advances were against the Word of God. Thus, she spearheaded a two-volume project, *The Woman's Bible,* in which she and seven other women commented on every text of the Bible that concerned women. Two other notable foremothers in feminist biblical interpretation were Angelina (1792–1873) and Sarah (1805–79) Grimké, daughters of a Quaker slaveholding family in South Carolina, who became ardent abolitionists and outspoken advocates for women's rights. When men attempted to silence them by quoting texts such as "women should be silent in the churches. For they are not permitted to speak, but should be subordinate, as the law also says" (1 Cor 14:34), they decided that they would learn Greek and Hebrew so that they could study the Bible in its original languages and thus be equipped to interpret the texts for themselves. A contemporary of the Grimké sisters was Belle Bumfree (1797–1883), better known as Sojourner Truth, a former slave who became a very influential preacher and advocate for women. Another notable figure was Sor Juana Inés de la Cruz (1648–95), a Mexican nun who was a prolific poet and writer. Despite attempts to silence her, she argued vociferously for women's right to an education and relentlessly challenged sexism. These are only a few examples of women who blazed the way for contemporary feminist biblical interpretation.

In the twentieth century, the social movement for women's rights sparked a new wave of feminism. Women biblical scholars, who were increasing in number, began to bring new questions to the interpretation of the Bible. They examined the Scriptures and the methods employed to interpret them for ways in which the texts were being used to oppress women. Some decided that the Bible was too thoroughly patriarchal to be liberating for women, and they urged women to abandon the Bible and biblically based religions. Others insisted that the Bible was still the Word of God and that what was needed were the right methods to interpret it. In this book we take the latter approach.

Why Feminist Interpretation of the Bible?

The rise in consciousness about women's treatment as second class in society and in the church is what has propelled efforts at understanding how the Bible can be either a help in countering such attitudes or an ally in the effort to keep women subordinate to men. While there have been many advances in women's rights, there is still a very long way to go before equality is achieved, both in society and in the church. A few examples of the inequities tell the story.

As of January 2015, only 20 of the 100 US senators and only 87 of the 435 members of the House of Representatives were women; as of September 2015, only six of the fifty states had female governors.[2] World-wide, only twenty-seven countries were led by women as of September 25, 2015.[3] Despite much progress since the turn of the millennium, still only one in five parliamentarians worldwide is female.[4] In the business world women have made inroads into middle-level management; slightly more than half of middle-level managers in the United States are women. But very few top business executives are women. Less than 3 percent of the CEOs of Fortune 500 companies are female.[5] In most other countries in the world, the gap is even larger.[6] When it comes to pay, women in the United States earn on average 77 cents for every dollar that a man earns for the same kind of work. Similarly, African American women earn only

---

2. See www.infoplease.com/ipa/A0768502.html and http://en.wikipedia.org/wiki/List _of_female_governors_in_the_United_States.

3. See www.guide2womenleaders.com/Current-Women-Leaders.htm.

4. See the United Nations Millennium Development Goals Gender Chart prepared in March 2014: http://unstats.un.org/unsd/mdg/Resources/Static/Products/Progress2014/Gender%20Chart%202014.pdf.

5. See www.womenonbusiness.com/new-us-women-in-business-statistics-released-by -catalyst.

6. See the Gender Gap Report 2013 of the World Economic Forum: www3.weforum.org/docs/WEF_GenderGap_Report_2013.pdf. This report notes that, out of the 110 countries studied in 2006-13, fully 86 percent have improved their performance in terms of gender equality. For 14 percent of the countries, however, the gender gap is widening (p. 7). There has been significant deterioration in countries such as Jordan, Kuwait, Mali, and Zambia, which were already at the lower end of the rankings (p. 35).

69 cents for every dollar African American men are paid, and Latinas earn just 58 cents on the dollar compared to Latino men.[7] Women are almost half the paid work force in the United States, but more than half of them are at or below the minimum wage. In the past it has been argued that women do not need to earn as much as men, since men are the breadwinners for the family. Today, however, approximately 28 percent of American families are single-parent families. More than 80 percent of these are headed by single mothers, who typically struggle to make ends meet.[8] In 2013 the poverty rate for single-mother families in the United States was 39.6 percent, nearly five times more than the rate for married-couple families.[9]

In terms of education, girls in the developed world have nearly equal access to education in both primary and lower secondary education. In the developing world, there has been progress toward parity at the primary level, but the gap is still great when it comes to girls in secondary education. The United Nations reports that poverty is the most important factor preventing girls and boys from attending school, but gender and location also play a role.[10]

The most disturbing statistics concern violence toward women. According to the data gathered by the World Health Organization, 30 percent of women worldwide have experienced intimate-partner violence.[11] This statistic is actually lower than the reality in many places, since incidents of domestic violence very often go unreported. Reports from ten different countries show that between 55 percent and 95 percent of women who had been physically abused by their partners had never contacted nongovernmental organizations, shelters, or the police for help.[12] The systematic rape of women has become a weapon of war. In 2011 a study done by the International Food Policy Research Institute at Stony Brook University in New York and the World Bank found that 1,152 women in the Democratic Republic of the Congo were raped every day—a rate equal to

7. Statistics are from a 2012 report from the U.S. Census Bureau. See www.huffington post.com/2013/09/17/gender-wage-gap_n_3941180.html.

8. See p. 23 of the U.S. Census Bureau report: www.census.gov/prod/2013pubs/p20-570 .pdf.

9. See https://singlemotherguide.com/single-mother-statistics.

10. United Nations Millennium Development Goals Gender Chart (see note 4 above).

11. Ibid. The three regions with the highest incidence of violence are South-East Asia (37.7 percent), Eastern Mediterranean (37 percent), and Africa (36.6 percent).

12. See http://domesticviolencestatistics.org/domestic-violence-statistics.

48 per hour.[13] Similar atrocities against women are currently happening in war-torn Syria.[14]

In the church, there are also many inequities. In some denominations, women are barred from ordained ministry and from positions of leadership and decision-making on the basis of their gender alone. In others, although women are ordained, they are assigned to the least influential posts, and they continue to be sidelined from decision-making bodies. The history of women disciples and leaders in earlier ages has, in many cases, been forgotten and, in some instances, deliberately suppressed. Sexism is still alive and well in most churches.

There is great need for communities of believers to engage the Bible in addressing these social and ecclesial realities. The Bible is not a neutral agent in our meaning-making. Depending on how the Bible is read, it can either reinforce sexism and violence toward women, or it can be a powerful force for change, helping believers to move toward becoming communities of equal disciples, where all the baptized, female and male, are regarded as equally made in God's image and likeness, equally redeemed by Christ, and equally empowered by the Spirit.

Womanists, Mujeristas, and Eco-feminists

From the beginning, feminists have asserted that it makes a difference whether one reads the Bible as a woman or as a man. Attention to gender perspectives in reading the Scriptures has been at the center of the endeavor. More recently, there has been a rise in consciousness that not only gender, but race, class, and culture are all determinative factors in how one understands the text. The realities of white, Western, educated women, who were the first to adopt the name feminist, are different in many ways from the realities of women who are from nondominant cultures in the United States or northern Europe. These are different yet from the realities of women in Asia, Africa, and Latin America. Moreover, the perspectives of women who are poor or illiterate are very different from those of women who are educated or financially secure. To draw attention to their differences in cultural and racial experiences, African American women in the United States began to call

---

13. See www.theguardian.com/world/2011/may/12/48-women-raped-hour-congo.

14. See www.dailystar.com.lb/News/Middle-East/2013/Nov-25/238863-rape-used-as-weapon-of-war-against-syria-women-report.ashx#axzz3FfnN9mGG.

themselves "womanists."[15] Likewise, some Hispanic women in the United States adopted the name *mujerista* (from *mujer,* Spanish for "woman"),[16] while others prefer the term "Latina feminists."[17] African, Asian, and Asian-American feminists also articulate the ways in which their perspectives differ from those of white feminists in the United States and northern Europe.

One other term that has gained prominence is "eco-feminism." Eco-feminists are those who connect the struggle for women's dignity with respect for all life, all of nature, in all of the cosmos. They take a holistic approach, understanding that we are all connected in one web of life, and that the well-being of one affects that of all. They see a link between human domination of nature and male subjugation of women, both of which are upheld by patriarchal systems. When working for the liberation of women, eco-feminists are also mindful of the dignity of the earth and all its inhabitants.

Today there is a great effort on the part of feminists from differing cultures around the globe to network with one another, to become more acquainted with the varying realities of one another, and to build bonds of solidarity to work for change together, worldwide. This book is written by a white, middle-aged, well-educated woman from a lower-middle-class family from Detroit, Michigan, a Roman Catholic sister, who is a professor of New Testament and vice-president and academic dean at a Roman Catholic school of theology and ministry, and who has had a great many opportunities to experience life with people in other parts of the world. I call myself a feminist and will continue to use that term throughout the book for convenience, but I will also incorporate insights from women of other cultures and hope that the interpretations given here can be a helpful source for reflection for women and men from cultures different from mine.

Feminists Come in Two Genders

The impetus for social equality for women and for feminist biblical interpretation and theology naturally originates with women. But women are

15. Alice Walker (*In Search of Our Mothers' Gardens: Womanist Prose* [New York: Harcourt Brace Jovanovich, 1967, 1983]) coined the term.

16. See Ada María Isasi-Díaz, *Mujerista Theology: A Theology for the Twenty-First Century* (Maryknoll, NY: Orbis, 1996).

17. María Pilar Aquino, Daisy L. Machado, and Jeannette Rodríguez, eds., *A Reader in Latina Feminist Theology* (Austin: University of Texas Press, 2002).

not alone in their efforts to build a more just society and church. There are many men who are sympathetic to women's concerns and who have committed themselves to walk with women on this journey. A feminist, to use Joan Chittister's definition, is a person who is committed to the humanity, dignity, and equality of all persons, to such an extent that she or he is willing to work for changes both in relationship patterns and in institutional structures to achieve this goal. The difference between a male feminist and a female feminist is that a man will never be able to reflect on women's experiences firsthand. He will always be something of an outsider. As familiar as he may be with women's experiences, he will never know what it is like to be discriminated against simply for being a woman. He might know from the inside another kind of discrimination, such as racism, if he is African American or Latino, for example, and this experience can help him relate to gender discrimination. Most feminists recognize that, while there is need for women to have their own space to share and to work together, it is also crucial to have men join in the struggle with women to undo the unjust structures that support sexism and to work together to build structures for a new egalitarian society and church.

Coming to Feminist Consciousness

It is not an easy journey to move from a patriarchal mind-set to a feminist one. It entails reimagining everything we thought we understood about our world and how it works, and about our faith and how we relate to God, one another, and our cosmos. It is as difficult a shift as it was for our ancestors to move from a geo-centered to a helio-centered understanding of the universe. The first scientists to propose that the earth revolved around the sun rather than vice versa were excommunicated, since this was thought to pose a threat to God's power! Similarly, it is very difficult to move away from a patriarchal worldview, in which it is accepted as normal that women are dominated by men, and that systems and institutions are organized and led by men. A feminist egalitarian worldview is one that envisions women and men in mutual relation, sharing power, calling forth one another's gifts, and regarding one another with equal respect and dignity.

What usually begins the process of letting go of patriarchy is a personal experience of discrimination that shocks one into having to confront the fact that all is not well. As in the process of death and dying, the first reaction can be one of fear and denial. A woman realizes that, if she begins down this road, it will demand a reordering of her world, changing the way she thinks and acts. There may be fear that such a move will threaten everything that one held dear in the past. But when a turning-point experience hits home deeply, one can no longer leave well enough alone.

The next stage is that one becomes outraged at the injustice. This can be a very difficult stage, since in most cultures women are socialized to be loving, sweet peace-builders. The image of an angry, confrontive woman is distasteful to most of us. And if we try to express our anger, we risk being misunderstood or dismissed. Our friends, family, and community members may not understand and may no longer want to be around us, just when we need the most support. Anger can be a very useful emotion, however, when channeled into creative action for transformative change. If we never became outraged at injustice, we would never have the impetus to work for change.

Usually, the next step is that our rage does not stay directed only at the one(s) who initially triggered the process. Once we see the discrimination toward us in one instance, we begin to see it everywhere. Sexism is like air pollution: seemingly invisible, it permeates everywhere. It often happens, then, that there is impasse, a dark night of the soul, where all the energy we put into trying to right the injustice seems to bear no results. Everything— our sense of self, our relationships, our place in our faith community and in the world—is all in turmoil, and there seems no viable way forward. Yet, neither is there any way to go back to what was before. The way forward usually comes through abandonment to God in contemplation. In a death-like experience, much like that of Jesus on the cross, we find that all we can do is faithfully place ourselves and our pain in the hands of God, who will free us for nonviolent, selfless, liberating action for the well-being of all. This breakthrough experience is much like that of giving birth. The only way forward to the new egalitarian worldview is through a kind of death. With the arrival of the new, however, the memory of the birth pangs fades, and liberating joy predominates (John 16:20-21).

How to Interpret the Bible from a Feminist Liberationist Perspective

Feminists have developed many methods for engaging the Bible as an ally in the construction of an egalitarian world and church. What follows is a sketch of a method that has been developed by Elisabeth Schüssler Fioren-za.[18] It involves seven steps.

1. *Begin with women's experience.* A feminist liberationist approach begins with analyzing real-life experiences of women, particularly ways in which women are oppressed. This step involves reading with "the mind, eyes, and heart of a woman."[19] It also means paying attention, not only to women's experience of gender discrimination, but also to inequalities based on race, culture, class, age, and ethnicity. It is also important to listen to the voices of women from many different contexts, for there is no universal "women's experience." Reflecting on women's varied experiences of oppression and liberation and their causes is the starting point.

2. *Identify the interpreter's social location.* A next step is to recognize that one's social location determines what lenses we bring to the text. A well-to-do white, well-educated man in North America will see a text very differently from a poor, illiterate woman of Mayan descent in rural Mexico. For example, in trying to understand the parable of the workers in the vineyard (Matt 20:1–16), a person of privilege who identifies with the workers who have spent the whole day laboring in the sun might wrestle with questions of entitlement and perceived injustice. However, a person who stands day after day in unemployment lines, and who reads from the perspective of the overlooked laborers standing all day in the marketplace waiting to be hired, will likely see in the parable a message of reassurance that God's grace is given equally to all and is not something to be earned.

3. *Ask: "Who says?"* A third step is to question who wrote the text, for whom, in what circumstances, and with what purpose. Here it is important to acknowledge that the books of the Bible have been written, for the most part, by men, for men, about men, and to serve men's purposes. Furthermore, the majority of the work of interpreting the Bible in biblical commentaries, sermons, and Bible studies has been done by white, Western, educated men. In using this step, we recognize the human element in the shaping of the traditions that we have received. While the Bible is revered as the Word of God, which authentically communicates God's desires for humanity, nevertheless, the instruments God uses are fallible humans. As Rosemary Radford Ruether asserts, we should not regard as "the Word

18. Elisabeth Schüssler Fiorenza, *Wisdom Ways: Introducing Feminist Biblical Interpretation* (Maryknoll, NY: Orbis, 2001).

19. The phrase "con ojos, mente, y corazón de mujer" is from the women of Coordinación Diocesana de Mujeres (CODIMUJ), of the Diocese of San Cristóbal de las Casas in the state of Chiapas, Mexico.

of God" any text that denies, diminishes, or distorts the full humanity of women.[20] Rather, whatever leads to life to the full for all (John 10:10), and in particular, whatever lifts up the oppressed, is truly God's word.

4. Evaluate: What does the text do? A next step is to evaluate what the text does to those who accept it. Does it reinforce domination and oppression? Or does it liberate for full life? For example, when a text such as "wives, be subject to your husbands" (Col 3:18) is read in the worship assembly, what is the effect? For a woman who is in an abusive relationship, it can be heard as justification for her husband to continue to batter her and for her to submit meekly. Such an interpretation is completely contrary to the liberating message that Jesus proclaimed. From a feminist perspective, another way of reading the text must be found in which God's desire for fullness of life for all and God's power for liberation are brought to the fore. With each text, evaluating what it does is an ongoing task. One cannot say what it does once and for all, but in each different situation this question must be asked again.

5. Unleash creative imagination. In addition to critical evaluation, it is necessary to engage all the powers of creative imagination to dream of a world in which equality and dignity of women is a fact. Without being able to envision such a world, we will not be able to create it. Drama, storytelling, music, art, dance, and ritual can all help to unleash the creative powers that can move us from possibility to reality.

6. Re-member and reconstruct. It is necessary not only to envision a new future but to retrieve the past. This step entails recovering women's history in the church and recalling that women have always been central to discipleship and mission. We bring forgotten female ancestors in the faith out from the shadows and seek their wisdom. Reading between the lines, we listen for the traces of women's voices that have been submerged. We look at the women mentioned in the Scriptures and think of them as only the tip of the iceberg. For example, if there is one woman named as a deacon (Phoebe in Rom 16:1) and one named an apostle (Junia in Rom 16:7), then there must have been many more whose names are now lost to us. Another strategy for reconstructing is to distinguish between what is being described in a text and what the biblical author is prescribing. For example, when Paul says, "Women should be silent in the churches" (1 Cor 14:34), we can recognize that women are, indeed, speaking in the assemblies, while Paul is prescribing that he wants this practice to cease. Rather than simply

20. Rosemary Radford Ruether, *Sexism and God-Talk: Toward a Feminist Theology* (Boston: Beacon, 1983), 19.

accept what Paul is prescribing, a feminist approach would be to investigate further what kinds of speech women were employing and who wanted them to be silent and why. One other strategy for re-membering is to envision women as present, even if they are not specifically mentioned. An example is the story of the feeding of the five thousand, in which neither Mark (6:44) nor Luke (9:14) mentions women. Matthew, however, concludes by saying that "those who ate were about five thousand men, besides women and children" (Matt 14:21). So, too, a feminist always asks, Where were the women? One last strategy is that, when there is mention of apostles, prophets, teachers, and preachers in the text, we should envision women who also exercised those ministries, not only the Twelve and the other male leaders.[21]

One other aspect of memory should not be lost. Not only are there traditions that are laudatory toward women that need to be retrieved, but there are also terrible stories, "texts of terror," as Phyllis Trible calls them, such as the abuse and dismemberment of the unnamed concubine in Judges 19. While some people think it best to delete such stories from memory, another liberative strategy is to remember and tell such stories, but with the very deliberate purpose of exposing the brutality of patriarchally approved violence against women and denouncing it with the insistence, "Never again!"

7. *Take action for transformative change.* Feminist liberationist biblical interpretation is not a method that remains an intellectual exercise. It insists that, after studying women's realities and analyzing the biblical text in the ways described above, the process must culminate in deliberate action aimed at transformation. Not only do we articulate a new vision, but then steps and strategies for making that vision a reality must be designed. Feminists work at changing relationship patterns on the personal level, as well as dismantling structures of domination.

All biblical interpretation is an art, not a formula that can be followed exactly so as to produce the correct meaning for all time. Feminist biblical methods of interpretation are no exception. It is not a matter of following these seven steps sequentially, but as Elisabeth Schüssler Fiorenza asserts, they are more like dance steps that interweave one another in various patterns. It is a lively tango that can energize us for a new world and church,

---

21. The use of a hyphen in "re-member" is intended to evoke the importance of realizing that women were among the members of disciples, missionaries, apostles, teachers, preachers, and so forth in the past and are still full members today. "Remember" without a hyphen is meant to invite the use of memory in two ways: both to recall the presence and contributions of women in the past, and to make them fully present now and in the future.

one in which women and men together can thrive in the fullness of life envisioned by Jesus.

The chapters that follow are a smorgasbord, a sampling of how to engage a feminist liberationist approach to the Bible. Woman Wisdom's banquet table awaits. While one may choose to dine there alone, it is usually more enjoyable to share the meal with friends. Questions at the end of each chapter can be used both for individual reflection and for group sharing about what you are tasting at Wisdom's Feast.

FOR DISCUSSION

1. What is your experience concerning gender inequalities and violence against women?
2. How would you identify the lenses you bring to biblical interpretation from your own social location? That is, what is your race, age, ethnic background, education, religious tradition, marital status, social status, and so forth?
3. On a scale from 1 to 10, how would you rate your level of feminist consciousness and commitment to feminism? What experiences have brought you to this point? Where would you like to be?

FOR FURTHER READING

Clifford, Anne. *Introducing Feminist Theology.* Maryknoll, NY: Orbis Books, 2001.

Habel, Norman C., and Peter Trudinger. *Exploring Ecological Hermeneutics.* SBLSymS 46. Atlanta: Society of Biblical Literature, 2008.

Isasi-Díaz, Ada María. *Mujerista Theology.* Maryknoll, NY: Orbis Books, 1996.

Junior, Nyasha. *An Introduction to Womanist Biblical Interpretation.* Louisville: Westminster John Knox, 2015.

Osiek, Carolyn. *Beyond Anger: On Being a Feminist in the Church.* New York: Paulist Press, 1986.

Schüssler Fiorenza, Elisabeth. *Wisdom Ways: Introducing Feminist Biblical Interpretation.* Maryknoll, NY: Orbis Books, 2001.

Trible, Phyllis. *Texts of Terror: Literary-Feminist Readings of Biblical Narratives.* Philadelphia: Fortress Press, 1984.

CHAPTER 1

Creation of the World and of Humankind

God created humankind in his image,
in the image of God he created them;
male and female he created them.
God blessed them, and God said to them, "Be fruitful and multiply,
and fill the earth and subdue it; and have dominion over the fish of the
sea and over the birds of the air and over every living thing that moves
upon the earth."

GEN 1:27–28

Then the LORD God said, "It is not good that the man should be alone;
I will make him a helper as his partner." So out of the ground the LORD
God formed every animal of the field and every bird of the air, and
brought them to the man to see what he would call them; and whatever
the man called every living creature, that was its name. The man gave
names to all the cattle, and to the birds of the air, and to every animal
of the field; but for the man there was not found a helper as his part-
ner. So the LORD God caused a deep sleep to fall upon the man, and
he slept; then he took one of his ribs and closed up its place with flesh.
And the rib that the LORD God had taken from the man he made into
a woman and brought her to the man. Then the man said,
"This at last is bone of my bones
and flesh of my flesh;
this one shall be called Woman,
for out of Man this one was taken."
Therefore a man leaves his father and his mother and clings to his wife,

and they become one flesh. And the man and his wife were both naked,
and were not ashamed.

GEN 2:18–25

Traditional Readings of the Creation Stories

The creation stories in Genesis 1–3 are often used to argue for women's inferiority and for their domination by men. Traditional readings see the creation of man as the paradigm, with woman created as an afterthought. Created second is often interpreted as being second best and inferior. For the woman to be created from the man's rib is seen as her deriving from the man, and therefore subordinate to him. The story of the entrance of sin into the world in Genesis 3 is often read as saying that woman is a temptress, the weaker sex, who capitulates first and thus is to be ruled over by man according to divine decree. We will take up Genesis 3 in the next chapter. In this chapter we study Genesis 1 and 2 and will see that, when read from a feminist perspective, these chapters tell of God's creation of woman as equally good and equally made in God's image, not to be ruled over by man but to be in harmonious partnership with one another to care for creation and to participate in God's ongoing creative activity.

Myth of Origins, Not Historic Event

First, it is important to realize that Genesis 1–3 does not describe actual historical events; rather, these chapters relate myths of origins. "Myth" does not mean that it is not true. On the contrary, myth expresses the *truth* of what we know to be and tells in story form how it came to be so. Myths bind people together at the deepest level, giving meaning to why things are the way they are. They help societies to know where they fit in the scheme of things and how to order their lives in community.

Every culture has its myths of origins. It is startling how many of the features of ancient Israel's creation stories are parallel to those in other ancient Mesopotamian creation accounts. There are, however, significant differences. While Babylonian creation myths also tell of humanity being made from clay and of human beings created in pairs, a distinct difference in Israel's creation stories is that human beings are not made to be slaves of the gods, but rather are made in the image and likeness of God (Gen 1:27) and share in God's creative activity.

Two Creation Accounts

It is easy to see that there are two different accounts of creation in Genesis 1 and 2, written in two very different styles, by two different authors. The first account, in Genesis 1:1–2:4a, is rhythmic and liturgical in nature, describing creation as a seven-day process, beginning with the creation of light and culminating with the creation of humankind on the sixth day, after which God takes a sabbath day to delight in it all. The second account, in Genesis 2:4b–25, begins with the creation of a human being, then describes how God fashions the plant and animal world, culminating in the creation of woman to be companion to the man. In the first account, God is called Elohim and seems distant from the creatures, creating by divine pronouncement. In the second, God is called Yahweh and is described in human terms, walking and talking with human beings. Most biblical scholars believe that the second account is the older of the two.

In 1878 Julius Wellhausen proposed that there were four sources—dubbed J, E, D, and P—in the Pentateuch, a hypothesis that has had wide acceptance by biblical scholars. In recent years, however, questions have been raised about the number of sources and their dating. Wellhausen thought that the "J" source, which uses the name Yahweh for God (called "J," from the German spelling *Jahweh*), dated to the ninth or tenth century BCE, originating in Judah, the southern part of Israel, and glorifying the monarchy created by David and Solomon. The "E" source calls God "Elohim" and features divine communications through dreams and angels. The "D" source pertains to the book of Deuteronomy and deals primarily with the covenant. The "P" (i.e., Priestly) source often uses "El Shaddai," usually translated "God Almighty," in the book of Genesis. This tradition is thought to have originated in Judah, with a school of priests who gathered together Israel's cultic and legal traditions during or shortly after the time of the Babylonian exile (597–538 BCE). This school is also thought to be responsible for bringing the various sources together to edit them into the Pentateuch after the exile.

The two sources thought to lie behind Genesis 1–3 are J and P. While today some scholars date the J source much closer to P, the important thing to know is that there are two different explanations at work in Genesis 1–3 for how creation came about and what God's intent is for humanity within creation. We will look first at Genesis 1:1–2:4a, from the P source, and then at Genesis 2:4b–25, from the J source.

Genesis 1:1–2:4a

The first creation story is majestic and rhythmic, emphasizing God's mastery over chaos, as God creates order and sets boundaries, placing all in right relation. From a "formless void" and a "face of the deep" covered in darkness, God creates a world in which light is separated from darkness, day from night, sky from the waters below, sea from dry land, sun from moon, with the whole earth teeming with vegetation and animals. After each new act, there is a refrain, "And God saw that it was (very) good" (vv. 4, 10, 12, 18, 21, 25, 31).

The Goodness of Creation Two very important theological affirmations emerge from this story. One is that the world and everything that God created is good. In fact, at the end of the sixth day, as God surveys everything that has been made, the final declaration is, "Indeed, it was very good" (v. 31). There is nothing that points to the world as evil or dangerous, or anything that human beings need to guard against. The whole of what God has done is a source of divine delight. God spends sabbath luxuriating in a love affair with the good creation.

A second affirmation in this story is that God is more powerful than the forces of chaos. When these forces arise again and threaten to destroy the good world that God has made, God is able to bring forth goodness once again. For a people emerging from the traumatic experience of exile, this story of God's power to put all in ordered goodness would have been a great comfort.

Male and Female Created in God's Image At the climax of the story God creates human beings in the divine image. Genesis 1:27 is poetic, constructed in three parallel lines:

> God created humankind [*ha'ādām*] in his image,
> in the image of God he created him [*'otô*];
> male and female he created them [*'otām*].

The first line speaks of humankind as one creature, *ha'ādām,* which means, literally, "earth creature" (the Hebrew word for earth is *'ădāmâ*). Line 2 repeats that humanity, regarded as one creature is created in the image of God. The pronoun is singular, *'otô,* "him," translated as a plural in the NRSV, rightly capturing that the pronoun has "a collective, common-gender sense."[1] The final line clarifies the idea that, although humankind is one, it comprises both male and female (now the pronoun is plural, *'otām,* "them"), created thus by God.

Genesis 1:27 thus affirms that male and female together are created in God's image. Despite Paul's statement that man "is the image and reflection of God; but woman is the reflection of man" (1 Cor 11:7), this is not what Genesis 1:27 says. Male and female together are created in the divine image. This is an astounding affirmation, given that, in other ancient Near Eastern religions, statues or images of the god were thought to make the god present to the worshipers. These handmade images usually took the form of an animal or a human being. Israel, by contrast, forbade the use of any images for God. It was in human beings that the presence of God was made manifest.

The Priestly writer may also have used the phrase "image of God" to counter the notion in other ancient societies, such as the Egyptians, that the king was the visible form of the deity on earth. Israel did not speak of its kings in this way. Rather, Genesis 1:27 uses the same language to speak of the special relationship to God enjoyed by humanity as a whole.

Fertility and Care for Creation Another way to understand what "the image of God" means is that, just as God is a creator, so human beings share in the ongoing divine creative work when they are "fruitful and multiply and fill the earth" (Gen 1:28). Moreover, from the same verse, just as God exercises sovereignty over all that is made, so human beings are given dominion over all the other living things on the earth. It is important to understand both parts of Genesis 1:28 in proper context. First, although the Priestly writer speaks of creation being finished after the sixth day (Gen 2:1-2), he also describes God as giving creation the power to continue to replenish itself. Plants and trees are created with every kind of seed and seed-bearing fruit (1:11-12); birds and sea creatures are blessed and told to be fruitful and multiply (v. 22). We know, too, from science that what God

---

1. Carol Meyers, *Rediscovering Eve: Ancient Israelite Women in Context* (New York: Oxford University Press, 2013), 70.

has set in motion is not a static, unchanging entity but one that continues to evolve and flourish. As we now know from the new cosmology, our universe flashed forth about 13.8 billion years ago, our solar system about five billion years ago, and it is ever-expanding. The creative work of God is ongoing, and human beings, as the image of God, participate in this continuing creation, not only by procreation, but in myriad ways of fashioning life anew. It is also important to remember, in an age where overpopulation is a concern, that the divine command in Genesis 1:28 belongs to the myth of origins and to primeval time. It is not a command meant to be carried out literally, applicable to all times and places.

A second way in which human beings are made in God's image is that they are given responsibility for all the other living things. While the verbs *kābaš* and *rādâ*, usually translated "subdue and have dominion," have often been interpreted as giving human beings free rein to exploit the earth and its creatures for human benefit, a proper understanding of this divine command is that human beings are to exercise care for all creation in the same way that the Deity does. Just as God delights in the goodness of creation and ensures its order and viability, so the human community is to do likewise.[2]

In sum, the first creation account, in Genesis 1:1–2:4a, emphasizes the goodness of creation, including the goodness of sexuality, the power of God over all that is made, and the entrusting to human beings, male and female together made in God's image, the ongoing care for the earth and all its creatures. Nothing in the story points to the superiority of the male. Humankind is spoken of as a unity, within which there is differentiation of male and female. There is nothing about "opposite sexes." The emphasis is on how humankind relates to God.

Genesis 2:4b–25

In Genesis 2 the focus shifts to how male and female relate to one another. This second account of creation, the older of the two, begins with God creating a human being, *ha'ādām*, from clods of earth[3] and breathing into its

2. See further Antoinette Collins, "Subdue and Conquer: An Ecological Perspective on Genesis 1:28," in *Creation Is Groaning: Biblical and Theological Perspectives*, ed. Mary L. Coloe (Collegeville, MN: Liturgical Press, 2013), 19–32.

3. Meyers, *Rediscovering Eve*, 71, notes that in Iron Age Israelite context the imagery is clods of sun-baked soil broken into clumps, not loose powdery dust.

nostrils the breath of life, so that it became a living being (v. 2:7). The story goes on to recount how God then created a garden and placed the human being in it to till it and keep it (v. 15). God then decides that it is not good for the human being to be alone. So God decides to make "a helper as his partner" (v. 18). This is a very important phrase, to which we will return shortly. The story continues with God creating out of the ground all kinds of animals and birds, which God brings to the man to see what he will call them. He names them all, "but for the man there was not found a helper as his partner" (v. 20). Finally, God causes a deep sleep to fall upon the man, and God takes one of his ribs and fashions it into a woman. "This at last is bone of my bones and flesh of my flesh!" exclaims the man (v. 23).

Woman as the Crown of Creation In some traditional interpretations of Genesis 2, the creation of the woman second and from the man's rib is read to mean that woman is second best and derivative from man and therefore should be subordinate to him. However, as Phyllis Trible has shown, there is another way to read this story.[4] The creation of woman is the result of a deliberate decision by God, not an afterthought. Moreover, the movement of the story in Genesis 2 is that God keeps improving on creation. At first there is no plant or greenery of the field (v. 5), so God creates a garden (v. 8). When there is no rain to water the garden (v. 5), God causes a stream of water to rise from the earth. Needing someone to till the ground (v. 5), God fashions a human being (v. 7). And when the human being needs a companion (v. 18), God creates woman (vv. 22-23). The literary structure of the story points to the creation of woman as the pinnacle of creation. Just as in the first creation account the climax is the creation of human beings as male and female (Gen 1:27), so in the second account, creation reaches its height with the fashioning of woman as partner to man.

"A Helper as His Partner" Many have understood the phrase "a helper as his partner" (v. 18) to mean that man is the paradigmatic human being and woman is designed simply to help him. Often this "help" has been understood as helping with procreation, as Ambrose and Augustine advanced. A study of the Hebrew words *'ēzer kĕnegdô* yields a different meaning. The word *'ēzer* is a noun that means "help, rescue." It occurs twenty-one times in the Hebrew Scriptures, with fifteen of these referring to the salvation

---

4. The analysis of Genesis 1-2 in this chapter is based largely on the work of Phyllis Trible, *God and the Rhetoric of Sexuality*, OBT (Philadelphia: Fortress, 1978), 72-143.

that comes from God. In Psalm 20, for example, it connotes indispensable aid in time of great danger:

> The LORD answer you in the day of trouble!
> The name of the God of Jacob protect you!
> May he send you help [*ʿēzer*] from the sanctuary
> and give you support from Zion. (Ps 20:1-2)

The word *kĕnegdô* is a preposition, which literally means, "according to what is in front of" or "corresponding to." Together, the words *ʿēzer kĕnegdô* mean "a help corresponding to himself" or "equal and adequate to himself." This phrase, then, describes the equal partnership, mutual strength, and correspondence that God designed for woman and man. Newer translations of Genesis 2:18, such as "helper as partner" (NRSV) and "suitable partner for him" (NAB), capture the literal meaning of *ʿēzer kĕnegdô* better than some of the older translations, such as "help meet" (KJV).

Mutual Correspondence of Woman and Man Some have thought that the creation of woman from the side of man indicates subordination of woman to man. Such a conclusion, however, would mean that man, having been created from the dust of the earth, should be subordinate to the ground! Instead, woman's creation from man's rib can be read as telling of their mutual correspondence to one another. The word *ṣēlāʿ* in Hebrew means "side," here usually translated "rib." Woman is made from the side of man, to stand alongside him as his equal. As the man's exclamation in v. 22 affirms, she corresponds to him exactly. She is strong just like him ("bone of my bones"), but also weak like him ("flesh of my flesh").[5]

There is also a word play in v. 23 that reinforces the oneness of the man and the woman. He declares, "This one shall be called woman [*ʾiššâ*], for out of man [*ʾîš*] this one was taken." The play on *ʾîš/ʾiššâ* emphasizes the sameness of the two human beings. It is important to note that the man does not name the woman at this moment; not until Genesis 3:20 does he name her "Eve, because she was the mother of all living." Naming does

---

5. Another interpretation is given by Ziony Zevit (*What Really Happened in the Garden of Eden?* [New Haven: Yale University Press, 2013]), who notes that nowhere else in the Bible does *ṣēlāʿ* mean "rib," but rather refers to side structures, which in a human being would be limbs. He proposes that the creation story is meant to explain the lack of a bone in the male penis, as it was taken to create woman. See also "Congenital Human Baculum Deficiency" by Scott F. Gilbert and Ziony Zevit at http://cabinetmagazine.org/issues/28/gilbert_zevit.php.

not indicate domination or power over another. As with the naming of the animals (2:19–20), this is an act that identifies the relationship between the creatures and the one naming them, not an act of domination.

Allusions to Genesis 1 and 2 in the New Testament

Galatians 3:28

There are two explicit allusions to Genesis 1 and 2 in Paul's letters. In Galatians 3:28 Paul quotes a baptismal formula, "There is no longer Jew or Greek, there is no longer slave or free, there is no longer male and female; for all of you are one in Christ Jesus." This declaration insists that all distinctions in societal status have no significance in the Christian community. That is, all are equally redeemed in Christ. Baptism does not erase these status markers, but it renders them unimportant in the Christian community. For Paul, this truth does not translate into social equality. Even as he says "there is no longer slave or free," he still advises slaves to remain slaves (1 Cor 7:21–24) and to remain subject to their masters (Col 3:22–25). Likewise, Paul does not advocate equality for women in social structures. He asserts that all human beings, created "male and female" (Gen 1:27), are equally redeemed in Christ, but for him that fact does not imply other kinds of equality.

1 Corinthians 11:2–16

Paul argues more extensively from Genesis 1 and 2 in 1 Corinthians 11:2–16. This passage is notoriously puzzling, since it is not clear what the precise pastoral problem was among the Corinthians. Some think that the issue concerns women not wearing veils while they were praying and prophesying in the assembly. Others think it has to do with hairstyles or proper dress. It can be confusing when English translations, such as NRSV, have "veiled" (vv. 5, 6, 7), whereas the Greek verb *katakalyptō* actually means "covered" and may not be referring to veils at all. Whatever the issue, Paul's argumentation rests on his reading of the creation stories. He first asserts, "I want you to understand that Christ is the head of every man, and the husband is the head of his wife, and God is the head of Christ" (1 Cor 11:3). While some biblical scholars think that Paul is arguing here for the headship of a husband over his wife, others think he is merely speaking about the order in creation. The word for "head" in v. 3 is *kephalē,* which can also be understood as "source," as in the headwaters, or source, of a river. Thus, Paul could simply be saying that man is the source of woman; that is, he was prior in creation and provides the material out of which she is created, as Genesis 2:21 asserts. Paul is not intending to say anything about domination or authority. He is concerned about order in the liturgical assembly, and he reminds the Corinthians of the order in creation. He elaborates this point again in v. 8, where he says, "Indeed, man was not made from woman, but woman from man."

In between, Paul alludes to Genesis 1:27, saying in v. 7, "For a man ought not to have his head veiled, since he is the image and reflection of God; but woman is the reflection of man." Notice that Paul has not quoted Genesis 1:27 accurately, where both male and female are made in God's image. Weaving this together with an allusion to Genesis 2:18, Paul says in v. 9, "Neither was man created for the sake of woman, but woman for the sake of man."

While in 1 Corinthians 11:8-9 Paul argues from Genesis 1:27 and 2:18 for the derivative and secondary status of woman, he makes a surprisingly different assertion in vv. 11-12, "Nevertheless, in the Lord woman is not independent of man or man independent of woman. For just as woman came from man, so man comes through woman; but all things come from God." Here Paul seems to contradict his previous statements, as he speaks of the interdependence and mutuality of man and woman. Moreover, his previous insistence on woman's derivation from man is relativized as he now talks about their common source from God. Paul finishes his admonition by arguing that nature teaches what is proper to do (v. 14) and that the Corinthians should also behave according to custom, in line with all the other churches (v. 16).

It is important to recognize that Paul adapts the Scripture quotations from Genesis 1 and 2 to fit the situation and the arguments he wants to present. We face a double task in looking at these texts: first, to determine the meaning in the original context of Genesis, then to decipher Paul's meaning in the context of his first-century Christian communities. Then we may ask questions about how the texts speak to our context.

John 1:1-18

Another important allusion to Genesis 1 in the New Testament is in the Prologue of the Gospel of John. The Fourth Gospel begins with the same words as Genesis 1:1, "In the beginning. . . ." Like Genesis 1, John 1:1-5 asserts that creation is good and happens by divine decree. But the evangelist implies that the creation story is not yet complete. Through the *Logos* ("Word") and the response of human beings to the Logos, God is bringing creation to its intended end. The Logos reveals God, and those who accept the Logos are given the power to become children of God (John 1:12). This birthing of God's children happens not through human desire or fleshly union, but by God's doing (John 1:13), as Genesis also says. In John's Prologue, all who receive the Logos become children of God. While not specifying "male and female" as Genesis 1:27 does, the Fourth Evangelist implies that there is no distinction between the sexes in the ability to be a child of God.

Conclusion

In the account of creation in Genesis 1, creation reaches its climax with the making of humankind, male and female, in God's image. The emphasis is on how humankind relates to God. Female and male together continue to represent the divine being by participating in the ongoing creation and by caring for the earth and all creatures. In the account in Genesis 2, creation reaches its pinnacle with the creation of woman. The emphasis is on how woman and man relate to one another. Both are created by divine intent; they are creatures equal to and corresponding to one another. Only woman and man prove to be adequate partners to one another. In neither account are female and male "opposite" sexes. In both there is a mutuality and harmony. It is possible that the final editors of the Pentateuch deliberately put these two accounts together in order to underscore the goodness of creation, including the goodness of human beings. Even after we read of how human limitation and freedom brought sinfulness into God's good creation in Genesis 3, the subject of our next chapter, we cannot forget the refrain of Genesis 1, "How good!"

As we have read the creation stories from a feminist liberationist perspective, we have found nothing that indicates inferiority of women or subordination of woman to man. However, it must be said that it is unlikely that the original writers of these stories would have envisioned equality and mutual partnership of women and men in their social world. They belonged to a thoroughly patriarchal world, in which domination of women by men would have been the norm. The text, however, takes on a life of its own, despite the original understanding of the authors. Meaning is created anew in the interaction between the reader and the text in a new time and place. The text does not always and everywhere mean the same thing, as we can see in the ways that Paul alters biblical texts, adapting them to address contemporary concerns. In an age in which the detrimental aspects of patriarchy have been exposed, these texts offer a hopeful vision for a harmonious and mutually empowering relationship between women and men, which God approves as "very good!"

FOR DISCUSSION

1. How have you experienced women being treated as inferior to men?
2. What would change in your family, workplace, and church if women were regarded as equally made in God's image?
3. What concrete step can you take toward creating an equal partnership between women and men in your context?

FOR FURTHER READING

Bird, Phyllis. *Missing Persons and Mistaken Identities: Women and Gender in Ancient Israel*. OBT. Minneapolis: Fortress Press, 1997.

Brueggemann, Walter. *An Introduction to the Old Testament: The Canon and Christian Imagination*. Louisville: Westminster John Knox, 2003.

Carol Meyers, *Rediscovering Eve: Ancient Israelite Women in Context*. New York: Oxford University Press, 2013.

Niditch, Susan. "Genesis." Pages 26–45 in *Women's Bible Commentary*, 3rd rev. ed. Edited by Carol A. Newsom, Sharon H. Ringe, and Jacqueline E. Lapsley. Louisville: Westminster John Knox, 2012.

Ruether, Rosemary Radford. *Women and Redemption: A Theological History*. Minneapolis: Fortress Press, 1998.

Trible, Phyllis. *God and the Rhetoric of Sexuality*. OBT. Philadelphia: Fortress Press, 1978.

CHAPTER 2

The Entry of Sin into the World and Its Aftermath

In the creation stories of Genesis 1 and 2, there is an overriding sense of the goodness of creation and God's joy and delight that is shared with the first human beings. In Genesis 3 everything goes awry. Written by the same author as Genesis 2, the next chapter narrates the disruption of God's good creation with the entry of sin into the world. Like the first two chapters of Genesis, chapter 3 also belongs to the myths of origins, explaining how pain and suffering and death came to be part of the world. Although both the woman and man are present in the story and have active roles, traditional interpretations have laid the lion's share of the blame on the woman.

Traditional Interpretations

In traditional interpretations of Genesis 3, the woman is seen as the weaker sex, gullible, and easily tricked by the serpent. Then, she is said to be a temptress, who leads the man astray. She is seen as the source of all evil. God's way of putting order back into the disrupted harmony is to declare that man is to rule over woman (Gen 3:16).

Early church fathers perpetuated such interpretations. Tertullian (ca. 160–235) blamed all women for the sin of Eve:

> Do you not know that you are Eve? God's sentence hangs still over all your sex and His punishment weighs down upon you. You are the devil's gateway; you are she who first violated the forbidden tree and broke the law of God. It was you who coaxed your way around him whom the devil

had not the force to attack. With what ease you shattered that image of God: man! Because of the death you merited, the Son of God had to die.[1]

Similarly, John Chrysostom (ca. 347–407) wrote, "The woman taught once, and ruined all. On this account . . . let her not teach. But what is it to other women that she suffered this? It certainly concerns them; for the sex is weak and fickle. . . . The whole female race transgressed."[2]

In many contemporary cultures, Eve still functions as a symbol of a temptress. A brand of cigarettes is labeled "Eve," in a time when smoking is viewed as socially unacceptable. Many advertisers use images of seductive women to lure potential buyers. For some Christians, Eve's sin provides a reason why women should not be ordained or entrusted with any kind of leadership in the church or in society. The image of seductress prevails when some believers insist that women priests would distract men at prayer.

Genesis 3: The "Fall" and Original Sin

In addition to the misplaced emphasis on Eve as the source of all sin, there are two other traditional interpretations of Genesis 3 that are not true to the biblical text. One is the notion that Genesis 3 narrates an irrevocable "fall" from grace, whereby human beings are hopelessly alienated from God, an alienation that could be reversed only by Jesus. This interpretation was developed by patristic and later scholastic theologians, based on Greek philosophy. The Old Testament itself does not advance any notion of a "fall," and it does not again mention Genesis 3. There are many texts in the Old Testament that depict humans as sinning, but also as able to repent, and God as ready to forgive (e.g., Deut 30:11–14; Ps 51). What Genesis 3 stresses is the free choice that God gives to human beings to be obedient or not, and the consequences of such a choice.

Another interpretation that arose in patristic times is the notion that Genesis 3 refers to original sin. Augustine (354–430) read Genesis 3 as depicting human beings as hopelessly enslaved to sin, and in conjunction with

---

1. *De cultu feminarum*, book 1, chap. 1.
2. Homily IX on 1 Tim 2:11–15 in *Nicene and Post-Nicene Fathers of the Christian Church*, vol. 12: *Saint Chrysostom: Homilies on Galatians, Ephesians, Philippians, Colossians, Thessalonians, Timothy, Titus, and Philemon* (ed. Philip Schaff; Grand Rapids: Eerdmans, 1957), 436, www.ccel.org/ccel/schaff/npnf113.v.iii.x.html.

his reading of Paul's letter to the Romans, he elaborated a theology of the hereditary nature of sin. In Romans 5:12-21 Paul is speaking about the new life in Christ that frees believers from sin and death. His argument moves to the greater from the lesser: Christ's gift of grace has a far more beneficial effect on humanity than the malevolent effect of Adam's sin. Paul's main concern is to contrast the universality of sin and death with the universality of life in Christ. He is not speaking about original sin, nor is Genesis 3. Nonetheless, this interpretation has remained popular.

A Feminist Reading of Genesis 3

There are four sections to the story in Genesis 3. First is the narration of the disobedience of the woman and the man (vv. 1-7), followed by the conversation with God about what they have done (vv. 8-13). Third, the consequences for their disobedience are detailed (vv. 14-19), culminating in their expulsion from Eden (vv. 20-24).[3]

Part 1: Human Disobedience (vv. 1-7)

The first section begins with the introduction of a serpent. The snake, along with the tree of life and the theme of searching for immortality, is a traditional element in many mythical stories of origins. The author of Genesis 3 was perhaps familiar with these stories. The hero in the Babylonian epic of Gilgamesh, after passing many tests, cannot do what is needed to attain immortality. Having been given a shoot from a plant that will rejuvenate him, he loses it to a snake, who swallows it. In the Mesopotamian legend of Adapa, the first man is allowed into the council of the gods, who offer him the bread and water of life, which would give him immortality and divine status. He thinks this is a trick, so he refuses, forfeiting his chance to be with the gods forever. Genesis 3 brings together these same mythical elements, as the serpent tempts the first couple to grasp at immortality and wisdom.

It is notable that the person who interacts with the snake is the woman, not the man. She is presented as the stronger character. Although the man

---

3. This structure and much of the ensuing interpretation are based on Phyllis Trible, *God and the Rhetoric of Sexuality*, OBT (Philadelphia: Fortress Press, 1978), 72-143.

is present with her (v. 6), it is she who acts as the spokesperson for both. The snake asks her about God's directive to both of them, "Did God say, 'You [plural] shall not eat from any tree in the garden'?" (v. 1). Her response is in the plural, "We may eat of the fruit of the trees in the garden; but God said, 'You [plural] shall not eat of the fruit of the tree that is in the middle of the garden, nor shall you [plural] touch it, or you [plural] shall die" (vv. 2-3). The snake's retort continues with plural pronouns, "You [plural] will not die; for God knows that when you [plural] eat of it your [plural] eyes will be opened, and you [plural] will be like God, knowing good and evil" (vv. 4-5).

Not only is the woman the spokesperson for herself and the man, but she is also portrayed as knowledgeable, articulate, and well-informed about God's command. She discusses theology intelligently, accurately conveying what God has said. She is perceptive, recognizing the goodness of the fruit, desiring the ability to distinguish good from evil, and she makes the active choice to eat it. Even though her husband is present, she acts independently, both in her theological discussion and in her taking the fruit. By contrast, the man is silent and passive. He is present but does not speak either to affirm or to contradict what his wife says. He does not theologize aloud as she does. He follows her lead and simply accepts the fruit. Contrary to contemporary gender stereotypes, the woman is the vocal and active agent, the man is passive and acquiescent. The point of the story is clear: both the woman and the man are present in the garden, both are tempted by the serpent, and both succumb. Both disobey God's command, and both are responsible for bringing sin into God's good creation. The first effect is that the nakedness and vulnerability of which they had not been ashamed in the pristine creation (2:25) is now something that makes them feel exposed and defenseless, something that must be covered up (3:7).

Part 2: Confrontation with God (vv. 8-13)

In the next section the man and woman are confronted by God, who calls them to accountability for what they have done. God is portrayed in a human form, strolling about in the garden, while the man and woman try to hide behind the trees. Whether God is simply enjoying an evening promenade or is searching for the human beings is not clear. The focus in this scene now shifts to the man, as God calls out to him and asks him, "Where are you?" (v. 9). When the man replies, he does not speak in the plural, as the woman did in the previous section. The oneness that they had enjoyed before their sin was committed is now shattered. He speaks for himself alone: "*I* heard the sound of you in the garden, and *I* was afraid, because *I* was naked; and *I* hid myself" (v. 10). When God presses him, asking, "Who told you that you were naked? Have you eaten from the tree of which I commanded you not to eat?" (v. 11), the man is defensive: "The woman whom you gave to be with me, she gave me fruit from the tree, and I ate" (v. 12). He first tries to blame the woman, and then points a finger at God for giving her to him. God then turns to the woman and asks, "What is this that you have done?" (v. 13). She, too, speaks for herself but does not try to implicate the man. She admits, "The serpent tricked me, and I ate" (v. 13). It is important to note that the woman rightly says it is the serpent who is the tempter, not she herself.

Part 3: The Consequences (vv. 14-19)

The next scene details the consequences of sin. Everything in creation is affected negatively by the transgression of the human beings. First, the serpent is cursed. There is now alienation between the snake and other animals. In addition, where there had previously been harmony between animals and human beings, now there is opposition (vv. 14-15). The consequences for the man are that he will have to labor hard in order to eat, tilling the ground by the sweat of his brow, and battling with thorns and thistles to gain produce from Earth that humans can eat. Having unsuccessfully grasped at immortality, he will return to the ground from which he came. Human sinfulness also has consequences for Earth itself, which, like the snake, is cursed (vv. 17-19).

The consequences for the woman stand at the center of those detailed for the serpent, the man, and Earth. According to Trible, three things befall the woman. First, childbirth becomes agonizing for her. Second, what was once mutual desire and delight between her and her man, now is not reciprocated. Third, not only is the former mutuality gone; worse yet, her man now rules over her.[4] In a close reading of the Hebrew text within the context of peasant life in Iron Age Israel, Carol Meyers understands 3:16 as explaining the hardships for women who had to bear many children so that there would be several viable offspring for cultivating the fields, caring for aging parents, and to inherit the land. At a time when only 50 percent or

---

4. Trible, *God and the Rhetoric of Sexuality*, 126-28.

less of the children born survived into adulthood, and as the risks to women escalated with each pregnancy, the last line of 3:16 expresses that the man overcomes woman's resistance to sexual relations. The man's mastery over woman is not in all aspects of life, but only with regard to sexual relations so that the agrarian household would have sufficient offspring.[5]

As Genesis 3 tells the story, none of these harmful consequences were part of God's original intent. The Creator made everything good and pleasing, existing together in harmony and delight. But God also gave human beings freedom to choose whether or not to perpetuate this divine design. Human creatures, both the man and the woman together, chose to act contrarily to what God had devised. Neither was more guilty than the other. Both ate the fruit. Neither was tempter of the other. It was the serpent who tempted them. When they succumbed, God's good order went awry, affecting the earth, its creatures, and human beings alike. The harmonious relations God had designed degenerated into opposition, struggle, and sinful domination. Unlike the creation stories of other ancient peoples, which tell of how the gods deliberately tried to keep human beings from attaining immortality, the author of Genesis puts the blame on human sinfulness.

Part 4: Expulsion from Eden (vv. 20-24)

In the aftermath of human disobedience, the man begins to exercise his dominion over the woman by naming her. Like many biblical names, it has a significance that matches what the person is. The Hebrew word *hawwah,* from which "Eve" derives, means "life," thus, the man names his wife "Eve, because she was the mother of all living" (v. 20). No naming of the man is narrated in Genesis. We have come to call him "Adam," based on the Hebrew word for "the human being," or "the man," *ha'ādām,* created by God in Genesis 2:7. There is a word play between *ha'ādām,* "the man," and *ha'ădāmâ,* "the earth," from which he is created. By the narrative logic of Genesis 2, however, *ha'ādām* should be understood as "the human being" or "the earth creature," until God creates woman (2:22). Then there is distinction between man and woman.

5. Carol Meyers, *Rediscovering Eve: Ancient Israelite Women in Context* (New York: Oxford University Press, 2013), 81-102. Her translation of 3:16 is: "I will make great your toil and many your pregnancies; with hardship shall you have children. Your turning is to your man/husband, and he shall rule/control you [sexually]."

In the next verse (v. 21), God is portrayed as a compassionate tailor, making clothing for the human beings out of animal hides. These will give far more protection than the fig leaves that the man and woman had sewn together for themselves (v. 7). Awareness of nakedness and vulnerability that entered human consciousness with their disobedience is an ongoing reality.

In the narrative, the man dominates from the point of disobedience forward. The woman is referred to as "his wife," not as a person in her own right (vv. 8, 20, 21). Moreover, the woman is not even included in God's pronouncement of expulsion from the garden: "'See, the man has become like one of us, knowing good and evil; and now, he might reach out his hand and take also from the tree of life, and eat, and live forever'—therefore the LORD God sent him forth from the garden of Eden, to till the ground from which he was taken. He drove out the man; and at the east of the garden of Eden he placed the cherubim, and a sword flaming and turning to guard the way to the tree of life" (vv. 22-24). Only the man is mentioned as being driven out of the garden, though the next chapter presumes that the woman is with him.

Ongoing Effects of Misogynistic Readings of Genesis 3

While some biblical texts blame the first man for bringing sin into the world, the more prevalent tradition is that woman is to blame. In the letter to the Romans, for example, Paul says, "Therefore, just as sin came into the world through one man, and death came through sin, and so death spread to all because all have sinned" (Rom 5:12). Occasionally the devil bears the brunt: "For God created us for incorruption, and made us in the image of his own eternity, but through the devil's envy death entered the world, and those who belong to his company experience it" (Wis 2:23-24). More typical is the statement of Ben Sira, written between 200 and 175 BCE: "From a woman sin had its beginning, and because of her we all die" (Sir 25:24). In 1 Timothy 2:11-15 we find the prohibition of women teachers, based on a skewed reading of Genesis 3:

> Let a woman learn in silence with full submission. I permit no woman to teach or to have authority over a man; she is to keep silent. For Adam was formed first, then Eve; and Adam was not deceived, but the woman was deceived and became a transgressor. Yet she will be saved through

childbearing, provided they continue in faith and love and holiness, with modesty.

This letter was not written by Paul himself, but rather by a leader who invoked Paul's name to deal with pastoral difficulties around the turn of the first century. His command that women not teach belies the fact that women were indeed teaching. One example is narrated in Acts 18:24-28, where Priscilla, along with her husband, Aquila, taught the Way of God more accurately to the eloquent preacher Apollos. The author of 1 Timothy disapproves of such and insists that women should be subordinate to men. He argues from the order in creation and from his interpretation of Genesis 3 that the first transgression was entirely on the shoulders of the woman. According to his logic, women's roles as Christian disciples are restricted to childbearing and mothering. It is important to note that this position is actually contrary to what Paul himself says. In a number of his authentic letters, Paul names women who are leaders in the Christian communities, even remarking that Phoebe, deacon of the church at Cenchreae, has been a leader of himself as well as many others (Rom 16:1-2; see below, chap. 6).

Order in Creation

There is another instance in one of Paul's genuine letters, 1 Corinthians 11:6-12, where he alludes to Genesis 1-3 as part of his argumentation for getting the community to follow his advice about a problem in the liturgical assembly. It is not clear exactly what the difficulty was, and it is equally unclear what Paul is asking them to do. Some scholars think the problem was that women in Corinth were rebelling against the custom of wearing veils. Others, who note that the words "veil" and "unveiled" are not in the Greek text,[6] think it concerns hairstyles. Paul criticizes men who pray or prophesy with "something hanging down from the head,"[7] that is, long

---

6. In vv. 5 and 13 the adjective *akatakalyptos,* usually translated "unveiled," literally means "uncovered." In vv. 6 and 7 the verb *katakalyptomai* means "to cover." It is usually translated "wear a veil." Those who think Paul is talking about hairstyles interpret *katakalyptomai* to mean covering the head with a proper hairdo. See v. 15, where Paul says a woman's hair "is given to her for a covering." The Greek word *peribolaion,* "covering," literally means "wrapper" and may refer to braided hair wrapped around the head.

7. This is a more literal translation of the phrase *kata kephalēs echōn* than that of the NRSV, "with something on his head."

hair (see also v. 14). Women, in contrast, were to have long hair, but neatly wrapped around the head. For some scholars, Paul's concern about hairstyles was that there be no blurring of gender distinctions. Others propose that Paul did not want the women to prophesy with loose hair and be mistaken for members of a pagan cult, for whom disheveled hair was a sign of a true prophet.

Whether the conflict was over head coverings or hairstyles, Paul uses a surprisingly egalitarian interpretation of Genesis 2 in vv. 11-12 to try to resolve it:

> [6]For if a woman will not veil herself, then she should cut off her hair; but if it is disgraceful for a woman to have her hair cut off or to be shaved, she should wear a veil. [7]For a man ought not to have his head veiled, since he is the image and reflection of God; but woman is the reflection of man. [8]Indeed, man was not made from woman, but woman from man. [9]Neither was man created for the sake of woman, but woman for the sake of man. [10]For this reason a woman ought to have a symbol of authority on her head, because of the angels. [11]Nevertheless, in the Lord woman is not independent of man or man independent of woman. [12]For just as woman came from man, so man comes through woman; but all things come from God. (1 Cor 11:6-12)

In vv. 11-12 Paul alludes to the order of creation of the first man and woman to insist, not on superiority of man over woman, but on their interdependence and mutuality. He then undercuts any argument for superior status based on derivation by asserting that "all things come from God."

This statement is confusing, however, when Paul opens his argument by saying that "man is the head of woman" (v. 3)[8] and that man is "the image and reflection of God; but woman is the reflection of man" (v. 7). Some scholars think that, with his other allusions to the creation accounts, Paul is using "head" in v. 3 to connote "source" or order in creation, not to argue for authority of men over women. The more usual interpretation is that Paul is alluding to Genesis 3:16, where the first woman is told that the man will rule over her. In v. 7, where he is alluding to Genesis 1:27, Paul does not deny that women are also created in God's image, but his silence on this half of the equation is troubling. And his assertions that "woman is

---

8. The word *anēr* can be translated either "man" or "husband"; similarly, *gynē* as either "woman" or "wife."

the reflection of man" (v. 7) and "woman [was created] for the sake of man" (v. 9) seem quite contrary to the egalitarian statements in vv. 11-12. Paul's uses of the Genesis texts in this instance seem contradictory. To bring his point home, he then appeals to the teaching of nature (vv. 13-15) and finally, to the customs observed in the other churches (v. 16).

Submission of Women to Men in Household Codes

One more allusion to Genesis 2 and 3 appears in the letter to the Ephesians:

> [21]Be subject to one another out of reverence for Christ. [22]Wives, be subject to your husbands as you are to the Lord. [23]For the husband is the head of the wife just as Christ is the head of the church, the body of which he is the Savior. [24]Just as the church is subject to Christ, so also wives ought to be, in everything, to their husbands. [25]Husbands, love your wives, just as Christ loved the church and gave himself up for her, [26]in order to make her holy by cleansing her with the washing of water by the word, [27]so as to present the church to himself in splendor, without a spot or wrinkle or anything of the kind—yes, so that she may be holy and without blemish. [28]In the same way, husbands should love their wives as they do their own bodies. He who loves his wife loves himself. [29]For no one ever hates his own body, but he nourishes and tenderly cares for it, just as Christ does for the church, [30]because we are members of his body. [31]"For this reason a man will leave his father and mother and be joined to his wife, and the two will become one flesh." [32]This is a great mystery, and I am applying it to Christ and the church. [33]Each of you, however, should love his wife as himself, and a wife should respect her husband. (Eph 5:21-33)

This text begins with a statement that is egalitarian, urging mutual submission to one another. But it quickly shifts to a command for wives to be subject to their husbands, evoking Genesis 3:16. This mandate is coupled with a command to husbands to love their wives (v. 25), as Christ loves the church, and to love them as they love their own bodies (v. 28). The section concludes with an allusion to Genesis 2:24, the culmination of the creation of woman, which emphasizes the oneness of the woman and the man. The man exclaims with delight in their sameness ("bone of my bones and flesh of my flesh," v. 23). Then follows an etiological explanation,

"Therefore a man leaves his father and his mother and clings to his wife, and they become one flesh" (v. 24). In Ephesians 5:32, however, the author applies the oneness to Christ and the church, rather than the husband and the wife. He concludes with one more admonition to the husband to love his wife as himself and to wives to fear their husbands.[9] The message is conflictual. While husbands are to love their wives, they are yet the masters to whom wives must submit. However benevolent the husband may be, the fact of women's subjugation remains. Patriarchy motivated by love is nonetheless patriarchy—an inequitable system that prevents the full flourishing of women and men.

As we work with how to appropriate this and similar texts today, it is important to know the historical contexts in which they were written. The prescriptions found in Colossians 3:18–4:1, Ephesians 5:21–6:9, and 1 Peter 2:18–3:7 are Christianized versions of household codes that were commonly known from the teachings of philosophers, moralists, and political thinkers from the time of Aristotle onward. They delineate lines of authority and obedience not only between husband and wife, but also between parents and children, and between master and slaves. Since the household was considered a microcosm of society, the ramifications for following these patterns went far beyond the individual home.

In the New Testament versions of the code, not only is the harmonious household a microcosm of society as a whole, but it also symbolizes the relationship between God and humanity. The church, as "the household of God" (Eph 2:19), would also shape its patterns of authority and obedience as in the family. However, what these codes uphold are not divinely revealed roles, but culturally determined mores of the ancient world. In an age where roles of women in society and church have changed dramatically, where many husbands and wives strive to share equally in the running of their household, or where many households are headed by single, divorced, or widowed women, it is important to see that the household codes embedded in the New Testament letters reflect the culture of the day and are not intended for all times and places.

Even in antiquity there may well have been women and men who regarded these codes as outdated. These texts presume that the head of the family is male and has sole authority. But women such as Phoebe (Rom

---

9. The Greek verb *phobeomai,* translated by the NRSV as "respect," literally means "to be/become afraid." It is also used for fear or reverence for God, e.g., Acts 10:35; 1 Pet 2:17; Rev 14:7.

16:1-2), Prisca (Rom 16:3-5; Acts 18), Lydia (Acts 16:14, 40), and Nympha (Col 4:15), some of them leaders of house churches, were active in preaching, teaching, evangelizing, and various other ministries. Given the reality that such women were fulfilling the roles of deacons and apostles, their communities could not have missed how anomalous were the admonitions in Ephesians 5:21-33, Colossians 3:18-19, and 1 Peter 3:1-6. It is especially ironic that the very same letter that advocates women's subjugation recognizes Nympha as head of a house church (Col 4:15). Such women may have quietly ignored the efforts to squeeze them into traditional roles inscribed in the household codes. Moreover, there would have been a goodly percentage of women in the Christian households who were slaves, divorced, or abandoned, and who disobeyed their pagan husbands; their lives were not at all that of the ideal Greco-Roman matron reflected in the codes.[10] The codes reflect a certain ideal image of hierarchical control by men, but the reality was something else.

Some scholars propose that these codes were embedded in Paul's letters in order to persuade outsiders, including imperial authorities (esp. 1 Pet 2:18–3:7),[11] that Christians were no threat to the state, that they subscribed to the same household structure as others. Others think there may have been some members of the communities who found it disturbing that the emerging leadership of women and slaves was disrupting the traditional patriarchal household and the household codes were an attempt to restore order. Still others propose that the early communities advocated maintaining this outward social structure, while understanding themselves to all have inner, spiritual equality in Christ.

Contradictions

One other observation is that these statements advocating women's subjugation to their husbands stand in tension with other passages where Paul speaks in egalitarian terms, for example, "There is no longer male and female; for all of you are one in Christ Jesus" (Gal 3:28), and where he rec-

---

10. Carolyn Osiek and Margaret Y. MacDonald, with Janet H. Tulloch, "Ephesians 5 and the Politics of Marriage," in *A Woman's Place: House Churches in Earliest Christianity* (Minneapolis: Fortress Press, 2006), 118-43, here 141-42.

11. In 1 Pet 3:6 the example of Sarah obeying Abraham and calling him lord is evoked rather than Gen 3:16. There may be an allusion to Gen 3, however, in v. 7, where the author asserts that woman is "the weaker sex."

ognizes women as coworkers and equal partners in ministry (see below, chap. 6). There seems to be a real contradiction in these texts, both supposedly written by Paul.

Some scholars resolve the difficulty by proposing that the letters to the Ephesians and Colossians, as well as the Pastoral Letters (1–2 Timothy and Titus),[12] which also have a number of restrictive statements about women, were written not by Paul himself but by a later disciple who wrote in Paul's name to invoke his authority. There are good arguments to support this hypothesis, based on differences in language, tone, style, and theology from his authentic letters. However, the assertion that Paul did not write Ephesians and Colossians does not resolve the difficulty of how to reconcile these texts with other more egalitarian texts; it only shifts the authorship. Moreover, Paul himself is not always consistent in his approach to women. While in many texts he esteems women's ministry and leadership, others show him to be quite shaped by the patriarchal mores of his day (e.g., 1 Cor 11:2–16; 14:34–46; see below, chap. 8).

Conclusion

We have seen that Genesis 3 is an etiological story, one that was intended to explain the presence of pain, suffering, and death in the world. It portrays both women and men as responsible for the dissolution of the harmony and goodness of what God created. The snake, not the woman, was the tempter. Both the woman and the man chose to be disobedient, and both bore the consequences. One of the consequences was that man began to rule over woman. Genesis 3 does not assert that domination of women by men was intended by God; rather, it was part of the fallout from sinful human choices. A number of other biblical texts cite or allude to Genesis 3 to perpetuate the subordinate status of women. None of these texts are prescriptions for how women and men are to relate in all times and circumstances. The nature of the texts and the historical situations in which they were written need to be considered, as well as the contemporary contexts in which they are appropriated. It is also important to remember that, in the Scriptures, many texts stand in contradiction to those that advocate the subordination of women.

---

12. Most scholars also include 2 Thessalonians among the deutero-Pauline letters.

FOR DISCUSSION

1. In your experience, how have women been regarded as temptresses or the weaker sex? What is your response to such characterizations?
2. What is your experience of being able to name yourself and name your own reality and your desires? Is it different for women than it is for men?
3. In what ways have you experienced men's domination over women? In what ways do you work to break down such domination?

FOR FURTHER READING

Bassler, Jouette M. "1 Corinthians." Pages 557-65 in *Women's Bible Commentary*, 3rd rev. ed. Edited by Carol A. Newsom, Sharon H. Ringe, and Jacqueline E. Lapsley. Louisville: Westminster John Knox, 2012.

Bird, Phyllis. *Missing Persons and Mistaken Identities: Women and Gender in Ancient Israel*. OBT. Minneapolis: Fortress Press, 1997.

Brueggemann, Walter. *An Introduction to the Old Testament: The Canon and Christian Imagination*. Louisville: Westminster John Knox, 2003.

Johnson, E. Elizabeth. "Ephesians." Pages 576-648 in *Women's Bible Commentary*, 3rd rev. ed. Edited by Carol A. Newsom, Sharon H. Ringe, and Jacqueline E. Lapsley. Louisville: Westminster John Knox, 2012.

Levine, Amy-Jill, ed., with Marianne Blickenstaff. *A Feminist Companion to the Deutero-Pauline Epistles*. FCNT 7. London: T&T Clark, 2003.

Niditch, Susan. "Genesis." Pages 26-45 in *Women's Bible Commentary*, 3rd rev. ed. Edited by Carol A. Newsom, Sharon H. Ringe, and Jacqueline E. Lapsley. Louisville: Westminster John Knox, 2012.

Trible, Phyllis. *God and the Rhetoric of Sexuality*. OBT. Philadelphia: Fortress Press, 1978.

Yee, Gale A. *Poor Banished Children of Eve: Woman as Evil in the Hebrew Bible*. Minneapolis: Fortress Press, 2003.

CHAPTER 3

Parables of Female Godliness

When one tries to speak of mystery, literal language does not serve. We must turn to metaphor, analogy, symbol, and figurative speech. So when Jesus spoke about God and the reign of God, he used parables and figurative language. Mark in fact says, "He did not speak to them except in parables" (Mark 4:34). No one image ever captures fully who or what God is. No figure of speech ever expresses totally what the reign of God is. Even when we put all the parables together, the composite mosaic of images still does not give us the whole picture.

Most Christians have grown up calling God "Father," and this form of address is most prevalent in liturgical prayers. While the Gospels depict Jesus teaching his disciples to pray to God as "our Father" (Matt 6:9; Luke 11:2) and show him speaking of and to God this way, "Father" is not the only image Jesus used for God. In the Gospel of Luke, for example, we find three instances in which Jesus tells parables that have a female image of God. Before examining those, we will first explore how parables communicate.

Popularity of Parables

Parables and figures of speech are abundant in the Bible, used even before Jesus' time. The prophet Nathan, for example, used a parable about a rich man who took a little ewe lamb that belonged to another man to get King

---

An earlier version of this chapter appeared in *Int* 56 (2002): 284-94 under the title "Beyond Trivial Tasks, Petty Pursuits, and Wearisome Widows: Three Lucan Parables (Luke 13:20-21; 15:8-10; 18:1-8)."

David to recognize and repent of his sin with Bathsheba (2 Sam 12:1–12). Isaiah told a parable about a vineyard to express divine disappointment over Israel's unfaithfulness (Isa 5:1–7). Ezekiel spoke in parables, using an eagle and a cedar tree to speak about messianic restoration (Ezek 17:1–10). Parabolic stories were also used by Jewish rabbis and in secular culture. As an astute teacher and preacher, Jesus recognized the power of this form of story to express the profundity of divine reality.

How Parables Communicate

Jesus' parables can seem deceptively simple, because he uses everyday images to capture his listeners' attention. To farmers, he speaks about planting seeds (Mark 4:1–9), weeds that infest a wheat field (Matt 13:24–30), and unexpected harvests (Luke 12:13–21). With fisherfolk, he talks about a net that catches all kinds of fish that will need sorting (Matt 13:47–50). To herders, he tells a story of a lost sheep (Matt 18:10–14) and one of a final separation of sheep and goats (Matt 25:31–46). A baker easily enters into a story about putting leaven in the dough (Luke 13:20–21). By using familiar, everyday situations, Jesus immediately has his audience's ear.

But as the story progresses, there is almost always a surprising twist. The story does not end as expected. Harvests produce a 100 percent yield—a physical impossibility! A farmer lets weeds grow alongside his wheat. A widow argues her own case before an unjust judge—and wins! These stories are paradoxical and puzzling. They upset the status quo. By turning one's expectations upside down, they invite the listener into mystery. As they do so, they give no easy answers.

This is another characteristic of Jesus' parables: they are left open-ended, so that the hearer is left to puzzle over their meaning. After Jesus tells the parable of the sower, the disciples ask him to explain it to them (Mark 4:10). Only twice in the Gospels does Jesus interpret a parable,[1] and it is most likely that these allegorical interpretations do not come from the lips of Jesus but represent the later thinking of his followers.[2]

Not only are parables open-ended, but they are open to diverse interpre-

---

1. The parable of the sower (Mark 4:13–20 // Matt 13:10–17 // Luke 8:11–15) and the parable of the weeds and the wheat (Matt 13:36–43).

2. For more detail, see Barbara E. Reid, *Parables for Preachers—Year B* (Collegeville, MN: Liturgical Press, 1999), esp. chap. 9.

tations. The parable in Luke 15:11–32, for example, has a significantly different meaning, depending on which character the hearer identifies with. If one stands with the younger brother, there is an invitation to seek forgiveness that cannot be earned. Persons who see themselves as the older brother are invited to let go of a sense of entitlement and of joyless resentment toward those who have not stayed on the straight and narrow. Those who identify with the father are challenged to be leaders who absorb the pain of humiliation and loss and who welcome the wayward with open arms. Still another angle is to stand with the invisible mother and daughters who are not mentioned in the story and to hear what those who are excluded from the picture might say. The important thing is to recognize that each of these messages is valid, and that changing times and contexts affect the meaning for each new situation. This is not to say that a parable can mean anything we want it to mean. It is important to study what it was likely to have meant in its original, first-century Jewish context in Roman-occupied Palestine and in the contexts of the evangelists' communities before we discern a meaning for today.

A Call for Transformation

The impact of Jesus' parables is that they call the hearers to change their minds, hearts, and actions. Accustomed ways of thinking or speaking about God and God's reign are broken open. Some of Jesus' parables are directed at his opponents, such as the parable of the wicked tenants (Mark 12:1–12), which offers to the political leaders who were seeking to put Jesus to death one more opportunity to be transformed. Others of Jesus' parables are directed to the crowds, and still others only to his disciples. In each case, there is an invitation to stretch the imagination and heart to embrace the divine mystery in new ways.

Female Images of God

With this understanding of the startling nature of the parables and their call for transformation, we turn to three parables in the Gospel of Luke that depict the divine image in female form: a bakerwoman (Luke 13:20–21), a woman searching for a lost coin (Luke 15:8–10), and a widow who confronts an unjust judge (Luke 18:1–8). The last two are unique to Luke; the first is found also in Matthew 13:33.

Divine Bakerwoman

> [20]And again he said, "To what should I compare the kingdom of God? [21]It is like yeast that a woman took and mixed in with three measures of flour until all of it was leavened." (Luke 13:20-21)

Most preachers and commentators on this parable focus on the small amount of yeast needed to leaven a whole loaf of bread. The connection is often made between the small number of Jesus' initial followers and the large, worldwide spread of the church that has resulted. But it is not at all clear that this was the focus of the original parable of Jesus. Neither Luke nor Matthew refers to the small amount of leaven, as does the version found in the Gospel of Thomas: "The father's kingdom is like [a] woman. She took a little yeast, [hid] it in dough, and made it into large loaves of bread. Whoever has ears should hear" (§96).[3] In the parable of the mustard seed, which precedes that of the leaven, Matthew notes that mustard "is the smallest of all seeds," in contrast to when it is grown and becomes the "greatest of all shrubs" (13:32). This, along with Paul's statement that "a little yeast leavens the whole batch of dough" (Gal 5:9; similarly 1 Cor 5:6), has made us inclined to focus on the small amount of yeast in Luke 13:33. However, neither in Luke's parable of the mustard seed nor in his parable of the leaven is size mentioned. Another point to keep in mind is that, at one stage of the tradition, the parables of the mustard seed and the leaven circulated separately and do not necessarily have the same point. The Gospel of Mark has the parable of the mustard seed (4:30-32), but not the parable of the leaven. Both are found in the Gospel of Thomas, but not together (§20 and §96). Luke's version of this parable may not be about small beginnings having great results.

Agitation for Transformation A different way of understanding the parable opens up when we look at what yeast does when inserted in bread dough. As a fermenting agent, it permeates the whole, making it rise and transforming its taste and substance into something desirable and nutritious. Jesus uses the metaphor "yeast" to warn his disciples about the corrosive influence of other teachers: "Beware of the yeast of the Pharisees and of Herod" (Mark 8:15; similarly Matt 16:6, 11-12). Luke elaborates that the

---

3. Translation by Marvin Meyer, *The Gospel of Thomas: The Hidden Sayings of Jesus* (San Francisco: Harper, 1992), 61.

leaven is "hypocrisy" (12:1). Similarly, Paul warns the Galatians not to be misled by false preachers, saying, "A little yeast leavens the whole batch of dough" (Gal 5:9). Jesus' parable urges his disciples to embrace the "yeast" of his teaching, which agitates for transformation toward the fullness of the reign of God.

Three Measures of Flour Another startling detail in the parable is the amount of flour that is used: three "measures." This is a huge amount—about fifty pounds! This same amount (expressed also as "an ephah") figures in several other Bible stories, including Sarah baking for the three heavenly visitors (Gen 18:6), Gideon preparing to receive an angel of God (Judg 6:19), and Hannah making the offering for the presentation of Samuel in the temple at Shiloh (1 Sam 1:24). What these three scenes have in common is that the large-scale baking signals a coming manifestation of God. Likewise, the gospel parable points to the work of the bakerwoman as a vehicle for divine revelation. Connecting the parable of the leaven with the episode in Genesis 18, when Sarah bakes with the same amount of flour for the three visitors who predict her pregnancy, the "idea of hiding yeast and of the dough rising on its own can suggest insemination and then pregnancy."[4] This metaphor points to the coming messianic age as in 2 Esdras 4:39-40 and Romans 8:22.[5] The huge amount of flour may also be meant to evoke the messianic age. Irenaeus says it was foretold that in messianic times "a grain of wheat shall bring forth 10,000 ears, and every ear shall have 10,000 grains" (*Adv. Haer.* 5.33.3-4).

Hiding the Yeast An odd detail is that the woman "hid" (*enekrypsen*) the yeast in the flour. The verb *(en)kryptō* is nowhere else used in a recipe for "mixing" dough. Other uses of the verb *kryptō* ("to hide") in Luke may provide a clue to its meaning in the parable. At 10:21, Jesus rejoices in the Holy Spirit and says, "I thank you, Father, Lord of heaven and earth, because you have hidden (*apekrypsas*) these things from the wise and the intelligent and have revealed them to infants." At 18:34, the twelve do not grasp what Jesus says to them about his coming passion: it "was hidden (*kekrymmenon*) from them." And when Jesus laments over Jerusalem, he says, "If you, even you, had only recognized on this day the things that make for peace!

---

4. Amy-Jill Levine, *Short Stories by Jesus: The Enigmatic Parables of a Controversial Rabbi* (New York: HarperOne, 2014), 124.

5. Levine, *Short Stories by Jesus,* 124.

But now they are hidden (*ekrybē*) from your eyes" (19:42). In each of these instances, full understanding of the mystery of the divine realm is hidden, and the one who is doing the concealing is God until the propitious time of revelation. The parable may also be pointing its hearers to see that God's reign, though seemingly hidden, "is present in the communal oven of a Galilean village when everyone has enough to eat."[6]

God Revealed in Female Form While baking might evoke traditional images of women working in the confines of their homes, or providing support through bake sales and other behind-the-scenes ministries, the parable takes us into a more provocative possibility. The divine revelation of the inbreaking of the reign of God in the person and ministry of Jesus is symbolized by the transformative action of the woman putting yeast in the dough. The godly bakerwoman can open the way for women to minister in all ways that cause the church and the world to rise and be transformed. For some members of the church, when women take on the ministries of leadership and decision-making, this agitating action seems a corruptive influence. Jesus' parable can serve as an invitation to see instead a manifestation of the divine in the ways women bake, bless, break, and share from the gifts given them.

Seeker of the Lost

[8]"Or what woman having ten silver coins, if she loses one of them, does not light a lamp, sweep the house, and search carefully until she finds it? [9]When she has found it, she calls together her friends and neighbors, saying, 'Rejoice with me, for I have found the coin that I had lost.' [10]Just so, I tell you, there is joy in the presence of the angels of God over one sinner who repents." (Luke 15:8–10)

I have yet to hear a preacher choose this little parable for the focus of a sermon. In the Revised Common Lectionary, we are given the whole of Luke 15 for the gospel selection on the Twenty-Fourth Sunday of Ordinary Time. In Luke 15 there are three parables, all of which follow the same structure, all of which make the same point, but with three different images. The first is the parable of the shepherd, who could be female or male,

---

6. Levine, *Short Stories by Jesus*, 126.

who searches for the lost sheep (15:3-7), and the third is the parable of the prodigal father who reaches out to his two lost sons (15:11-32). It is always one or both of these parables that preachers choose to speak about. Feminist sensibilities alert us to the fact that the parable of the woman searching for the lost coin is equally important for opening us up to the God who seeks us.

A Parable for Leaders The introductory verses of the chapter tell us that Jesus directed these three parables at the Pharisees and scribes who were grumbling about the way he was welcoming and eating with tax collectors and sinners (15:1-2). By framing the parables this way, Luke points us toward the characters of the shepherd, the woman, and the father as exemplars for leadership. Outside of their literary context these parables can be open to other interpretations, as mentioned above. But for our purposes, we will follow Luke's direction and see what the parables may say about how leaders are to be.

A God Who Seeks the Lost It is easy for believers to see in the figure of the shepherd an image of God and a model for religious leaders. One of the most beloved psalms speaks of God as a shepherd, who leads us on right paths (Ps 23). And in the Old Testament, many of Israel's leaders were shepherds, for example, Moses and David. In several instances, the prophets take religious leaders to task, calling them shepherds who look after their own interests instead of caring for the sheep (Jer 23; Ezek 34). Likewise, in a church that speaks of God as Father more often than any other title, and who addresses its leaders similarly, it is not hard to see in the father in the third parable an image of God and a model for religious leadership. The second parable invites us to stretch our imaginations to allow the woman who searches for the lost coin to serve as an equally good image of God and for a leader in the church.

Costly Love One of the aspects of divine love that the parable shows is the great extent to which God will go to find and restore the lost. The woman spends much time, energy, and money in her search for the lost coin. Houses in first-century Palestine were dark, with small, high windows, since people lived primarily outdoors and used their homes only for storage and sleeping. So the woman must light a lamp, using up precious oil, while she tries to catch a glint from the coin. Floors in houses were packed dirt, or sometimes made of cobblestones. In either case, it would

45

be difficult to find a coin that had become lodged under a stone or covered over with dirt. The woman sweeps diligently and searches carefully for however long it takes to find the precious coin. In this detail, she is like the shepherd, who expends great energy searching over rocky terrain, hoisting the heavy, wayward animal on his shoulders, and bringing it back to the fold. She is also like the father, who watches and waits long days and nights, absorbing the insults and pain from one son who squanders his inheritance, and from the other who sees himself as a slave. All three figures speak of a divine love that is willing to pay any price to draw back the beloved lost one.

Joy Compounded Another feature in all three parables is the communal joy and celebration over the finding of the lost. When the woman has finally located the coin, she, like the shepherd and the father, calls together her friends and neighbors to share her joy. This celebration is an image of the heavenly rejoicing over repentant sinners (vv. 7, 10).

The three parables also emphasize that what is lost is so precious that it cannot be let go. A sheep is a very valuable animal. Even if there are ninety-nine others, no effort can be spared in finding the errant one. Similarly, a father will never let go a son without doing everything possible to bring him back. Just so, a woman entrusted with care of the household will never casually toss off the loss of a drachma. So God passionately seeks out each precious person that goes astray, never resting until that one lets herself or himself be found and brought back into the divine embrace. The divine joy and celebration that ensues take on heavenly proportions!

Misguided Interpretations It is curious that many preachers and biblical scholars fail to see the parallels between the parable of the searching woman and the other two in the trilogy and often veer off into misguided interpretations, some of which are tinged with sexism. Some depict the woman searching for the lost coin as miserly[7] or her action as trivial, important only to her women friends.[8] Some think of the ten coins as pocket change for her to spend on trinkets. Such misinterpretations have no basis in the text and fail to take into account the realities of women in first-century Palestine. Women had charge of the household finances and took

---

7. Joseph A. Fitzmyer, *The Gospel according to Luke X–XXIV*, AB 28A (Garden City: Doubleday, 1985), 1080.

8. The Greek nouns in v. 9—*philas*, "friends," and *geitonas*, "neighbors"—are feminine.

pride in their careful management of the home.[9] Most were very poor, living at a subsistence level. To lose a drachma could mean the difference between being able to feed the family for a day or going hungry. Any woman in such a situation would go to whatever lengths necessary to find a coin worth a day's wage.[10]

Another misinterpretation is that the lost coin was part of a set of decorative coins on a bridal headdress or a necklace. This approach makes the coin valuable because it is part of the woman's dowry, or because the whole necklace loses its value if it is missing one coin. The problem is that we have no evidence for such customs in first-century Palestine. It is a modern practice of nomadic Bedouin women to wear jewelry made from strings of coins. Among the thousands of coins that have been excavated from the time of Jesus, there is no evidence that coins were used in this decorative way in antiquity.

Wisdom Incarnate One other aspect of the parable of the searching woman is that there are echoes of the actions of Woman Wisdom, who seeks out the simple among human beings (Prov 1:20-23; 8:1-5) and invites all to her banquet (Prov 9:1-11). Jesus, as Woman Wisdom incarnate, seeks out the lost, welcomes tax collectors and sinners, and invites all to his table. Any who minister in his name are invited to do the same.

A Godly Widow Pursuing Justice

[1]Then Jesus told them a parable about their need to pray always and not to lose heart. [2]He said, "In a certain city there was a judge who neither feared God nor had respect for people. [3]In that city there was a widow who kept coming to him and saying, 'Grant me justice against my opponent.' [4]For a while he refused; but later he said to himself, 'Though I have no fear of God and no respect for anyone, [5]yet because this widow keeps bothering me, I will grant her justice, so that she may not wear me out by continually coming.'" [6]And the Lord said, "Listen to what the unjust judge says. [7]And will not God

9. Carol Scherstsen LaHurd, "Rediscovering the Lost Women in Luke 15," *BTB* 24 (1994): 66-76.

10. See further Susan Praeder, *The Word in Women's Worlds: Four Parables*, Zacchaeus Studies, New Testament (Wilmington: Glazier, 1988), 36-50.

grant justice to his chosen ones who cry to him day and night? Will he delay long in helping them? [8]I tell you, he will quickly grant justice to them. And yet, when the Son of Man comes, will he find faith on earth?" (Luke 18:1-8)

This parable, found only in the Gospel of Luke, paints a vivid picture of two opposing characters. In searching for what the parable says about God, most preachers and biblical scholars focus on the judge and see him as a negative example of what is not godlike. In cultures where God is thought of as a powerful male, it is understandable that people would expect the judge to be the figure for God. But the parable itself makes it clear that he is not, when the judge twice asserts that he has neither fear of God, nor respect for any persons (vv. 2, 4). A simple solution is that it is the widow who exemplifies godly action. In her persistent pursuit of justice, she is like God, who always sides with the poor and is relentless in her quest for right relation.

Layers of Interpretation Most biblical scholars recognize that the final form of Luke 18:1-8 includes not only Jesus' original parable but interpretive layers added by Luke. It is likely that vv. 1 and 6-8 represent later reflections by Jesus' followers, and that the verses closest to what Jesus said are vv. 2-5.[11] A favorite theme of the Third Evangelist is prayer,[12] but this focus is probably Luke's interpretation, not the point that Jesus was making. Many people follow Luke's lead and hear in the parable an urging to be persistent in prayer. But what emerges if we follow this line is a story that seems to say that if we, like the widow, just badger God long enough, God will finally relent and give us what we ask. We know from experience that this does not work! In addition, this interpretation offers a disturbing theology of prayer, which goes contrary to the way Jesus describes God as eager to give us everything we need (Luke 11:9-13).[13]

Persistent Pursuit of Justice If we begin with v. 2, we find a widow who is not persistent in prayer but who goes to court day after day after day,[14] insisting

11. For details on the redactional layers, see Barbara Reid, *Parables for Preachers—Year C* (Collegeville, MN: Liturgical Press, 2000), 227-36.

12. See Luke 3:21; 5:16; 6:12; 9:18, 28, 29; 10:21-23; 11:1-13; 22:32, 39-46; 23:46.

13. See also Sir 35:14-19, which assures that God "is not deaf to the wail of the orphan, nor to the widow when she pours out her complaint."

14. The verb *ērcheto*, "kept coming," is in the imperfect tense, indicating repeated past action.

that justice be done. We are not told the nature of the wrong done to her. It is startling for a woman to be arguing her own case. The usual thing would be for her nearest male relative to advocate for her. Perhaps it is he who is doing her wrong! Whatever the situation, the woman persists, despite the equally stubborn refusal of the judge.

The impasse is finally broken, not because the judge has had a change of heart—he repeats that he still neither fears God nor has respect for any human being (vv. 2, 4)—but he gives the widow the justice she wants so that she will not haul off and give him a black eye (v. 5)! Many Bible translations render the verb *hypōpiazein* metaphorically, e.g., "wear me out" (NRSV),[15] but the verb is a boxing term that means literally "to strike under the eye."[16] This ludicrous image of a powerful judge cowering before a determined widow causes us to laugh aloud. At the same time, the point is deadly serious.

The Godly One From this angle, it is the woman who is the godly one, who does not lose heart as the judge refuses her tireless attempts to rectify an unjust situation. In her persistence for justice, we see an icon of Jesus, who offered unending opportunities for repentance to those who opposed him, and whose power rested in speaking and pursuing truth.

A number of modern-day examples of such persistent widows come to mind. The Madres de la Plaza de Mayo—the widows, mothers, and sisters of the men who disappeared in Argentina's dirty war of the 1970s—continue to march in front of the Casa Rosada, the president's residence, in Buenos Aires, demanding to know the fate of their loved ones. Their actions contributed to the downfall of the military dictatorship. Similarly, Women in Black, a worldwide movement that began in Israel in 1988, confronts injustice, war, and other forms of violence through demonstrations, vigils, and educational actions. Such persistent actions have their roots in the Women's International League for Peace and Freedom, which began just after World War I.

Taming an Unconventional Widow With his attempt to place the emphasis on persistent prayer, rather than persistent demands for justice, Luke has

15. Similarly, KJV: "lest by her continual coming she weary me."

16. BDAG, 1040. Paul uses the term with this meaning in 1 Cor 9:26-27, "I do not fight as if I were shadowboxing. No, I drive *[hypōpiazō]* my body and train it." The NAB comes closer to the literal meaning: "lest she finally come and strike me"; NJB has: "or she will come and slap me in the face."

also tried to tame a disturbing image of an unconventional woman who intrudes in traditionally male spaces, doing things usually reserved to men. He preserves Jesus' startling parable, but by adding v. 1, he tries to evoke the image of Anna, who spent eighty-four years fasting and praying in the temple (Luke 2:36-38). Luke favors women who persist in prayer; he is not so keen on having them step into other arenas. Jesus, in contrast, seemed to have no trouble with women crossing such boundaries to persist in godly actions for justice.

The Importance of Female Images of God

The parables that offer us images of God as a woman who transforms bread dough with yeast, who diligently searches for the lost, and who persistently acts for justice until it is accomplished are not the only instances in the Bible where we find female images of God. In the Old Testament we find Moses warning the Israelites not to forget "the God who gave you birth" (Deut 32:18). The prophet Isaiah speaks of God being like "a woman in labor" when birthing the renewed Israel after the exile (Isa 42:14), and of God's tenderness like that of a mother consoling her child (Isa 49:15; 66:13). Isaiah 66:9 and Psalm 22:10-11 portray God as a midwife, drawing Israel forth from the womb. In Psalm 91 God's care for human beings is said to be like that of a mother eagle for her brood (v. 4). Jesus uses this same image when he laments over Jerusalem (Luke 13:34). In the book of Job we find both male and female language for the Creator, as God asks Job, "Has the rain a father, or who has begotten the drops of dew? From whose womb did the ice come forth, and who has given birth to the hoarfrost of heaven?" (Job 38:28-29).

These examples show that female images of God are biblically based, and that they serve equally well as male images to speak about God. What is important about female imagery for the divine is that it opens us further to the God who is beyond gender, and the Christ who has transcended gender. It also helps us to remember that our language for God is not literal, but figurative. A very important consequence is that, when God is spoken of in female terms, it enables us to see that women as well as men are made in the divine image and likeness, as Genesis 1:27 asserts. It also helps us to recognize the ways in which the divine is revealed in female experience, such as birthing, nurturing, baking, leading the search for the lost, and persisting in quests for justice. Such imaging opens us to ways of seeing Christ and his mission fully embodied by female disciples as well as male, so that no arena of ministry would be closed to women. A gender-inclusive church could then lead the way to dissolve the persistent inequities between women and men in so many other arenas of life, for example, government, health care, wages, education, to name a few.

FOR DISCUSSION

1. What is your experience of praying with female images of God?
2. How do the images of God as bakerwoman, diligent householder, and persistent widow speak to you?
3. Why is it important to use both female and male images to speak of and to God?

FOR FURTHER READING

Grey, Mary C. *Introducing Feminist Images of God.* IFT 7. Cleveland: Pilgrim Press, 2001.

Johnson, Elizabeth A. *She Who Is: The Mystery of God in Feminist Discourse.* New York: Crossroad, 1992.

McFague, Sallie. *Models of God: Theology for an Ecological, Nuclear Age.* Philadelphia: Fortress Press, 1987.

Moody, Linda A. *Women Encounter God: Theology across the Boundaries of Difference.* Maryknoll, NY: Orbis Books, 1996.

Ramshaw, Gail. *God beyond Gender: Feminist Christian God-Language.* Minneapolis: Fortress Press, 1995.

CHAPTER 4

Mary: Prophet of a New Creation

Mary, a Model for Women

Mary, the mother of Jesus, has traditionally been held up, especially in Catholic circles, as the model for women. A traditional reading of the Annunciation (Luke 1:26-38) sees her as wholly passive, submissive, and compliant to God's will. The image of Mary as a sweetly submissive maiden has been used to reinforce subordination of women and to fuel male projections about the "ideal woman." At times, Mary has been regarded as almost divine, as she is thought to embody all the female characteristics of the godhead, which find little expression in the predominantly male images of God.

Mary appears only briefly in the Gospels,[1] but in Luke and John she plays a very significant role. In this chapter we will focus on the scenes of the Annunciation and the Magnificat in Luke 1:26-38, 46-55. In chapter 9 we will reflect on her role in two key episodes in the Gospel of John: the wedding feast at Cana (2:1-11) and the crucifixion (19:25-27). In the Lucan texts, Mary is a powerful prophet who voices God's dream for well-being for all creation. In the Johannine scenes, Mary is witness and midwife of a new creation.

---

1. Mark 3:20-21, 31-35; 6:1-6; Matt 1:16, 18-25; 2:11; 12:46-50; 13:54-58; Luke 1:26-56; 2:1-7, 16, 19, 22-38, 41-52; 8:19-21; 11:27-28; John 2:1-11; 19:25-27; Acts 1:14. See further, Raymond E. Brown, *Mary in the New Testament: A Collaborative Assessment by Protestant and Roman Catholic Scholars* (Philadelphia: Fortress, 1978).

The Annunciation: Mary's Prophetic Call

[26]In the sixth month the angel Gabriel was sent by God to a town in Galilee called Nazareth, [27]to a virgin engaged to a man whose name was Joseph, of the house of David. The virgin's name was Mary. [28]And he came to her and said, "Greetings, favored one! The Lord is with you." [29]But she was much perplexed by his words and pondered what sort of greeting this might be. [30]The angel said to her, "Do not be afraid, Mary, for you have found favor with God. [31]And now, you will conceive in your womb and bear a son, and you will name him Jesus. [32]He will be great, and will be called the Son of the Most High, and the Lord God will give to him the throne of his ancestor David. [33]He will reign over the house of Jacob forever, and of his kingdom there will be no end." [34]Mary said to the angel, "How can this be, since I am a virgin?" [35]The angel said to her, "The Holy Spirit will come upon you, and the power of the Most High will overshadow you; therefore the child to be born will be holy; he will be called Son of God. [36]And now, your relative Elizabeth in her old age has also conceived a son; and this is the sixth month for her who was said to be barren. [37]For nothing will be impossible with God." [38]Then Mary said, "Here am I, the servant of the Lord; let it be with me according to your word." Then the angel departed from her. (Luke 1:26-38)

Biblical scholars recognize that the Annunciation to Mary is very similar in form to other annunciations of birth stories in the Bible,[2] such as that of Ishmael (Gen 16:7-13), Isaac (Gen 17:1-21; 18:1-15), Samson (Judg 13:3-20), and John the Baptist (Luke 1:13b-20).[3] These stories generally contain five elements: (1) appearance of angel; (2) fear; (3) heavenly message giving reassurance, the child's name, and the child's significance in salvation history; (4) objection; and (5) sign from God. But the Annunciation to Mary also fits another form, that of a prophetic call story. The elements are similar to those of an annunciation of birth story, but the scene has an additional purpose.

2. The following analysis is taken in large part from my essay "Women Prophets of God's Alternative Reign," in *Luke-Acts and Empire: Essays in Honor of Robert L. Brawley*, ed. David Rhoads, David Esterline, and Jae Won Lee, PTMS (Eugene, OR: Pickwick Publications, 2010), 44-59.

3. See Raymond E. Brown, *The Birth of the Messiah* (New York: Doubleday, 1977), 155-59, 292-96.

The Vocation of a Prophet

Before examining more closely the Annunciation scene as a prophetic call story, first it is important to understand what the vocation of a prophet is. Prophets are not fortunetellers. They are vessels of communication between God and the people. They are keenly attuned both to God's longing for well-being for all of creation and to the cries of the people. They have a two-pronged mission: to denounce wrongdoing and injustices that prevent the full flourishing of God's people and all creation, and to announce the way toward a fuller realization of God's reign. We now turn to Mary's call to exercise such a role.

Prophetic Call

Like the prophets of old, Mary's encounter with God's messenger comes in the midst of everyday life. Moses, for example, was tending the sheep of his father-in-law, Jethro, when God's angel appeared to him in a flame of fire out of a burning bush (Exod 3:1-12). Likewise, Amos was a simple herdsman and dresser of sycamore trees when God took him from following his flock and called him to prophesy to Israel (Amos 7:14-15). So too, Mary was an ordinary Galilean girl in the midst of making wedding plans when God's messenger appeared to her.

Authentic prophets always resist God's call. Moses objected that he was "slow of speech and slow of tongue" (Exod 4:10). Jeremiah protested that he was too young (Jer 1:6). Amos insisted, "I am no prophet, nor a prophet's son" (Amos 7:14). Isaiah retorted, "I am a man of unclean lips," living among "a people of unclean lips" (Isa 6:5). In like manner, Mary objects that what she has heard from Gabriel is impossible (Luke 1:34). Prophets know that what God asks of them is beyond their human capabilities.

The prophet's objections are always met by assurances of God's help. In the case of Moses, for example, God also empowers his brother, Aaron, saying, "I will be with your mouth and with his mouth, and will teach you what you shall do" (Exod 4:15). Moses' sister Miriam is also a prophet who exercises her gifts along with her two brothers (Exod 15:20). To Jeremiah, God affirms, "Do not be afraid. . . . I am with you to deliver you" (Jer 1:8). Isaiah is given a seraph who touches his lips with a live coal, declaring that his guilt has departed and his sin is blotted out. So then he is able to respond "Here am I! Send me!" (Isa 6:5-8). Mary, like Isaiah and Ezekiel (Isa

6:1 and Ezek 2:2), upon whom God's Spirit came, is given the assurance that the Holy Spirit will come upon her and that the power of the Most High will overshadow her (1:35). Nothing, she is told, is impossible for God (1:37).

Another reason why prophets resist their call is that prophets always experience suffering in the exercise of their mission. Jesus remarks in Luke 13:34 that Jerusalem always kills the prophets. Not all prophets are literally put to death for their prophesying, but all experience some measure of rejection and revilement. Because a prophet's vocation includes denouncing wrongdoing and injustices, she or he always encounters opposition from the ruling powers, who benefit from the oppression of others. They will take whatever measures necessary to silence the prophet. In a later scene, Luke alludes to Mary's suffering when Simeon says to her, "A sword will pierce your own soul" (2:35).[4]

The final reassurance given to Mary by Gabriel is that the Holy Spirit will empower her and that her child will not be called illegitimate, but "holy" and "Son of God." A further sign to her is that her kinswoman, Elizabeth, who has been barren, is also with child, "for nothing is impossible with God" (1:37). Trusting that God is faithful, Mary assents to the call.

Proclamation of God's Rule

[46]And Mary said,
"My soul magnifies the Lord,
    [47]and my spirit rejoices in God my Savior,
[48]for he has looked with favor on the lowliness of his servant.
    Surely, from now on all generations will call me blessed;
[49]for the Mighty One has done great things for me,
    and holy is his name.
[50]His mercy is for those who fear him
    from generation to generation.
[51]He has shown strength with his arm;
    he has scattered the proud in the thoughts of their hearts.
[52]He has brought down the powerful from their thrones,
    and lifted up the lowly;

---

4. Joseph A. Fitzmyer (*The Gospel according to Luke I-IX*, AB 28 [Garden City: Doubleday, 1981], 430) notes that this is an allusion to the sword of discrimination in Ezek 14:17, pointing toward the difficulties Mary will have as a result of her son's mission.

> [53]he has filled the hungry with good things,
>   and sent the rich away empty.
> [54]He has helped his servant Israel,
>   in remembrance of his mercy,
> [55]according to the promise he made to our ancestors,
>   to Abraham and to his descendants forever." (Luke 1:46–55)

Mary's prophetic work involves not only giving birth to the one who will claim the throne of his ancestor David and who will rule forever (1:32–33), but also proclaiming what this rule of God will be like (1:46–55). The scene takes place in the home of Elizabeth and Zechariah, where Mary both assists her elder kinswoman and is mentored by her to recognize everything as blessing, even in the most difficult of circumstances. In the scene of the Visitation (Luke 1:39–45), Elizabeth declares a threefold blessedness: "Blessed are you among women, and blessed is the fruit of your womb" (1:42), "and blessed is she who believed that there would be a fulfillment of what was spoken to her by the Lord" (1:45). As rumors and doubts swirl around her when her pregnancy becomes evident, Mary is strengthened by Elizabeth's assurance that all is blessed, all is holy, despite God's incomprehensible ways.

Mary then lifts her voice to sing out a vision of what the world would be like if God's desire for well-being for all were fulfilled. She follows in the footsteps of other female prophets—Miriam, Hannah, Judith, and Deborah—who proclaimed God's victorious power in song and dance.[5] Prophets not only declare oracles, but they also engage in "intercessory prayer, dancing, drumming, singing, giving and interpreting laws, delivering oracles on behalf of YHWH (sometimes in ecstasy, sometimes demonstratively), resolving disputes, working wonders, mustering troops and fighting battles, archiving their oracles in writing, and experiencing visions."[6]

---

5. Five women in the Old Testament are explicitly identified as prophets: Miriam (Exod 15:20), Deborah (Judg 4:4), Huldah (2 Kgs 22:14; 2 Chr 34:22), the unnamed woman with whom Isaiah fathers a child (Isa 8:3), and Noadiah (Neh 6:14). In addition, there are references in Joel (3:1-2) and Ezekiel (13:17) to daughters who prophesy, and 1 Chronicles 25:4-6 speaks of Heman, who directs his sons and daughters in musical prophecy. The Talmud adds Sarah, Hannah, Abigail, and Esther to those women recognized as prophets. In the New Testament, there is Anna (Luke 2:36-38), the four virgin daughters of Philip (Acts 21:9), and the women prophets of Corinth (1 Cor 11:5). A false woman prophet appears in Rev 2:18-28.

6. Wilda C. Gafney, *Daughters of Miriam: Women Prophets in Ancient Israel* (Minneapolis: Fortress, 2008), 6.

The parallels between Mary's song and the songs of Miriam (Exod 15:1–21),[7] Judith (Jdt 16:1–16), and Deborah (Jdg 5:1–31) make it impossible to miss the subversive nature of the Magnificat.[8] Miriam, identified as a prophet in Exodus 15:20, sings and dances, with tambourine in hand, exulting in God's triumph over the Egyptians. She leads the people to understand their experience of liberation as a gift from God and to further imagine—and thus be able to achieve—a new future in the land of God's promise.[9] Judith and Deborah likewise lead their people in a victory hymn after being freed from the terror of their enemies. These songs are not sweet lullabies; they are militant songs that exult in the saving power of God that has brought defeat to those who have subjugated God's people. In the same vein, Mary's song declares the overthrow of Roman imperial ways and the triumph of God's reign. Familiarity with the Magnificat from its frequent use in religious contexts, as well as the tendency to interpret Mary as sweet, docile, and utterly compliant, can cause contemporary readers to miss the subversive power of Mary's song. The Guatemalan government, however, recognized its revolutionary potential and banned the public recitation of the Magnificat during the civil war in the 1980s.

Lord, Savior, Mighty One

One of the ways in which Mary's prophetic proclamation challenges Roman imperial powers is in the titles that she uses for God: Lord *(kyrios)*, Savior *(sōtēr)*, and the Mighty One *(ho dynatos)*. Each of these titles evokes claims that were made by Caesar and counters them. There are many known instances, both literary and archaeological, where the title *kyrios* is attributed to the emperor. One example is found in the *Discourses* of Epictetus, where the emperor is referred to as *ho pantōn kyrios kaisar,* "lord emperor over all" *(Disc.* 4.1.12). Luke shows that he is aware that the emperor had appropriated this title for himself in Acts 25:26, where Festus refers to the emperor

---

7. It is likely that the entire Exodus hymn was led by Miriam, and not simply v. 21, which mirrors v. 1. That women were the ones who would lead victory songs and dancing is reflected in 1 Sam 18:7. See further George J. Brooke, "A Long-Lost Song of Miriam," *BAR* 20 (1994): 62–65.

8. More frequently noted are the parallels between Mary's song and Hannah's song (1 Sam 2:1–10).

9. Irene Nowell, *Women in the Old Testament* (Collegeville, MN: Liturgical Press, 1997), 52.

as *ho kyrios*. To counter this claim, Mary clearly asserts in the opening line of the Magnificat that God is *ho kyrios*. Luke reinforces this name by using *kyrios* for God and Jesus some two hundred times in Luke and Acts. Luke also contrasts the manner in which the Gentiles exercise their lordship with that of Jesus. "The kings of the Gentiles," Jesus says, "lord it over [*kyrieuousin*] them, and those in authority over them are called benefactors. But not so with you; rather the greatest among you must become like the youngest, and the leader like one who serves" (Luke 22:25-26).

Mary also calls God *sōtēr,* "Savior" (v. 47), another title the Roman emperors attributed to themselves. Julius Caesar, for instance, was described as "the god made manifest . . . and common savior of human life." Augustus was called "a savior who put an end to war" and "savior of the entire world."[10] Throughout the Third Gospel, these terms are used repeatedly of Jesus, God's true agent of salvation.[11]

The third title, *ho dynatos,* "the Mighty One" (v. 49), is also used of God in the Septuagint (the Greek translation of the Hebrew Scriptures), for example, in Zephaniah 3:17 and Psalm 89:9. Divine might, however, is shown to be far different from that of Rome. God's power is might that protects the most vulnerable, as Gabriel assures Mary (1:35). It is the power such as resided in Elijah and John the Baptist, "to turn the hearts of parents to their children, and the disobedient to the wisdom of the righteous, to make ready a people prepared for the Lord" (Luke 1:17). It is the power of the Spirit that impels Jesus throughout his mission (Luke 4:14) to do good and to heal[12] and to cast out unclean spirits (Luke 4:36). Jesus' "deeds of power" are meant to bring repentance (Luke 10:13) and to cause all his disciples to acclaim him as the "king who comes in the name of the Lord" as he enters Jerusalem (Luke 19:37).[13]

By naming God as *ho dynatos,* "the Mighty One," the Magnificat sets the stage for the way in which Jesus embodies God's power, namely, as a contrast to imperial power. This point is brought to a climax when, at the end of the gospel, Cleopas and his companion (who may have been a

10. For further references, see Steve Walton, "The State They Were In: Luke's View of the Roman Empire," in *Rome in the Bible and the Early Church* (Grand Rapids: Baker Academic Books, 2002), 27 n. 86.

11. Luke is unique among the Synoptic evangelists in his use of *sōtēr,* "savior" (Luke 1:47; 2:11; Acts 5:31; 13:23) and *sōtēria,* "salvation" (Luke 1:69, 71, 77; 19:9; Acts 4:12; 7:25; 13:26, 47; 16:17; 27:34; 28:28).

12. So also Luke 5:17; 6:19; 8:46; Acts 10:38.

13. This power is also given to Jesus' disciples: Luke 10:19; 24:49; Acts 1:8; 4:33; 6:8.

woman) declare that Jesus was "a prophet mighty [*dynatos*] in deed and word before God and all the people" (Luke 24:19).

Mary's acclamation of God as "Lord," "Savior," and "Mighty One" is prophetic speech that is a direct affront to Roman imperial claims. What she declares of God is embodied in her son, God's ultimate prophet.

Slavery and Servitude vs. Service

In v. 48 of the Magnificat, Mary repeats what she has said to Gabriel at the Annunciation (1:38): that she is God's servant (literally "slave," *doulē*). She is not the servant of Caesar, only of God. She says covertly what Peter and the apostles say overtly to the high priest in Acts 5:29: "We must obey God rather than any human authority." The term *doulē* also calls to mind that enslavement would be the fate of any who dared to rebel against Rome. Luke has noted that Mary was from Nazareth (1:26), a town located only a few short miles from Sepphoris, whose inhabitants revolted at the death of Herod in 4 BCE and who were enslaved in punishment (Josephus, *J.W.* 2.68; *Ant.* 17.289). Another means of enslavement was through Roman imperial economic practices. Many people were incapable of meeting the excessive demands of tribute, temple taxes and offerings, tithes, and other debts and were forced to sell lands and family members into debt slavery. Mary subverts the system of enslaving subjected peoples by presenting herself as an empowered person who chooses to serve. She is not a person upon whom servitude is imposed. This ethos is further embodied in Jesus' mission, as he declares himself to be one who serves (Luke 22:27), and who makes the deliberate choice to risk the consequences of imperial backlash for his liberating proclamation and actions.

Humiliation

There is another significant challenge to Roman imperial values in vv. 48 and 52. In contrast to powerful elites, who delight in humiliating those whom they dominate, God "looks upon" *(epeblepsen)* Mary's "humiliation" *(tapeinōsis),* with the intent of alleviating her affliction. The same combination of divine "looking upon" *(epiblepō)* an individual's humililation *(tapeinōsis)* with a merciful intent is found three other times in the Septuagint. In 1 Samuel 1:11 Hannah prays for God to look upon *(epiblepō)* the misery *(tapeinōsis)* of God's servant *(doulē)* and grant her a male child (1 Sam 1:11). Likewise, in 1 Samuel 9:16 God reveals to Samuel the one whom he is to anoint to be ruler over Israel to save them from the Philistines, "for I have seen [*epiblepō*] the suffering [*tapeinōsis*] of my people." Judith implores God to "have pity on our people in their humiliation [*tapeinōsis*], and look kindly [*epiblepō*] today on the faces of those who are consecrated to you" (Jdt 16:19). The resonances of these texts with the Magnificat create the expectation that God delights in relieving suffering that comes through humiliation,[14] quite the opposite of the ruling powers in the imperial system, who impose humiliation on their subjects. Elizabeth also voices how God delights in taking away humiliation when she exclaims, "This is what the Lord has done for me when he looked favorably on me and took away the disgrace I have endured among my people" (1:25). Mary's song declares that, not only has God done this for Mary, but God lifts up all the humiliated *(tapeinous,* v. 52).

The verb *tapeinoō* is also used a number of times in the Septuagint to refer to the sexual humiliation of a woman, as in the case of the rape of Dinah (Gen 34:2), the abuse of the concubine of the Levite (Judg 19:24; 20:5), Amnon's rape of Tamar (2 Kgs 13:12, 14, 22, 32), and the ravishing of the wives in Zion and the maidens in the cities of Judah by the enemy (Lam 5:11).[15] The Magnificat voices the dream that women will have no more fear of sexual humiliation by men who overpower them, that rape by occupying imperial forces will no more be used as a tool of subjugation.

Mercy and Meals

Another way in which divine power differs from that of imperial Rome has to do with food distribution. While the Roman Empire relied on military might, fear, and economic domination to maintain power, the divine

14. In two other instances *tapeinōsis* refers to affliction suffered by barren women, which God alleviates by giving them a son. In Gen 16:11 God heeds the affliction *(tapeinōsis)* of Hagar, and she conceives Ishmael. In Gen 29:32 God sees the affliction *(tapeinōsis)* of Leah, and she bears Reuben. These references shed less light on Luke 1:48, since Mary's affliction is not caused by barrenness, but by her conception of a son outside the bounds of patriarchal marriage arrangements.

15. Jane Schaberg (*The Illegitimacy of Jesus: A Feminist Theological Interpretation of the Infancy Narratives* [San Francisco: Harper & Row, 1987], 100) points out these references. See also Deut 21:14; 22:24; Isa 51:21, 23; Ezek 22:10-11.

Mighty One exudes mercy (vv. 50, 54) by bringing down the powerful from their thrones and lifting up those humiliated (v. 52), and by filling the hungry and emptying the rich (v. 53). It is not a simple reversal of fortunes for which Mary longs, but a leveling of the distribution of goods and power. She envisions a simultaneous movement of relinquishment on the part of those who have power, privilege, and status, and an empowerment of those who have not.

Luke frequently speaks of divine mercy *(eleos)*. It is manifest in the birth of a son to Elizabeth (1:58), and in the promise of a savior (1:71) who will bring light to those who "sit in darkness and in the shadow of death" (1:79). Jesus embodies this divine mercy by healing people afflicted with leprosy (17:12-13) and blindness (18:38-39). He teaches his disciples to be merciful by loving enemies, doing good, and giving to those who beg, without expecting recompense (6:27-36). This teaching subverts imperial ways of violent retaliation. Jesus tells a lengthy story about a hated Samaritan who embodies this kind of mercy, and he exhorts his followers to "go and do likewise" (Luke 10:37). He also tells a parable about a tax collector who went home justified after praying in the temple for mercy (18:13-14).

Another manifestation of divine mercy is filling up those who are hungry. As Warren Carter has shown,

> Food was about power. Its production (based in land), distribution, and consumption reflected elite control. Accordingly, the wealthy and powerful enjoyed an abundant and diverse food supply. Quality and plentiful food was a marker of status and wealth . . . that divided elites from nonelites. It established the former as privileged and powerful and the latter as inferior and of low entitlement. The latter struggled to acquire enough food as well as food of adequate nutritional value. For most, this was a constant struggle. And it was cyclic whereby most dropped below subsistence levels at times throughout each year. Food, then, displayed the injustice of the empire on a daily basis.[16]

As Mary sings of filling up the hungry, she subverts the imperial system that keeps nonelites struggling and starving, while elites enjoyed the abundance that the imperial propaganda touted as one of the gifts of the Roman Empire to its citizens. Throughout the rest of the Gospel we see

---

16. Warren Carter, *The Roman Empire and the New Testament: An Essential Guide* (Nashville: Abingdon Press, 2006), 109-10.

Mary's son setting about this agenda of filling up the hungry, as the Lucan Jesus is portrayed so very often in meal settings.[17]

When Mary sings of God sending the rich away empty, she introduces a theme that runs strongly throughout the gospel. In an empire where 2-3 percent of the population possessed most of the wealth, and where the majority constantly struggled to sustain a subsistence-level existence, Mary articulates an end to economic structures that are exploitative and unjust. She speaks of a time when all will enjoy the good things given by God. Throughout the Gospel, the Lucan Jesus frequently warns about the dangers of riches (12:16-21; 16:13, 19-23; 18:25). The ideal presented in Acts is that no one is in need (2:42-47; 4:32-34).

Portrait of the Ideal Woman

In the way Luke portrays Mary's actions and words, he subtly challenges the portrait of the ideal woman in the Roman imperial world, who was always under masculine control. When Mary is introduced in Luke 1:26, there is no mention of her father or her fiancé; rather, she is identified in relation to her town, Nazareth. She interacts freely with God's messenger, asking questions and answering for herself, without the control of a husband or father. Furthermore, she is outside the bounds of the ideal marriage and articulates her submission to God, but not explicitly to her husband. We also find Mary traveling from Nazareth to Judea to visit Elizabeth (1:39), without any mention of a companion or guardian.[18] While in some aspects Luke portrays Mary as contrary to the ideal image of a submissive woman of her day, there are other ways in which she does conform. Mary's prophetic proclamation is uttered not in a public place, which is reserved to men, but within the confines of a home (1:40).[19] It is

17. At times he is host (Luke 9:10-17; 22:14-20), while at other times he is a guest (5:30; 7:36; 10:38; 14:1; 19:7). At many of these meals Jesus challenges the assumptions of the Roman imperial world and offers an alternative vision of God's reign.

18. The popular fourteenth-century writer Ludolph of Saxony *(Vita Domini nostri Jesu Christi ex quatuor evangeliis)* solved what appears to be a most unorthodox situation by asserting that a train of virgins and angels accompanied Mary to protect her.

19. Elizabeth also conforms to the ideal for pregnant women, remaining five months in seclusion after conceiving (1:24). Her prophetic speech when naming her child and conveying God's message of grace takes place in a family gathering (1:59-66). Anna is the exception, who prophesies in a more public space in the temple.

her son who will bring out into the open the themes sounded in private in the Magnificat when he announces his mission in the synagogue at Nazareth (4:18-19). Throughout his Gospel, Luke gives a double message with regard to women. He depicts the majority of his female characters as silent and passive, staying behind the scenes and choosing the "better part" by listening silently, not engaged in ministries of diaconal leadership (Luke 10:38-42; see below, chap. 8).[20] However, while women in Luke seem outwardly to accommodate to the empire, inside their homes they equip their children and family members with stories and songs that envision an alternative rule to that of Caesar.

Conclusion

The Mary who is depicted in the texts we have examined in the Gospel of Luke is not a meek, passive, submissive woman. She discerns and faithfully responds to God's call without the mediation of a man. She is a bold prophet who utters a powerful proclamation of what life is intended to be in God's design. When her words are echoed in those of her son, one cannot help but conclude that it was she who taught him to think and act as a prophet. She is presented as the model disciple, who hears and acts on God's word. In this respect, she is an example not only for women, but for men as well. She is not divine but is utterly attuned to God, as well as to her people, deeply contemplative as she ponders everything in her heart (2:19, 51) and obediently responds to what God asks of her.

FOR DISCUSSION

1. How does the image of Mary as prophet speak to you?
2. What does the Magnificat call you to do, both individually and in your faith community?
3. What was your experience when you first sensed a call from God?

20. See further Barbara E. Reid, *Choosing the Better Part? Women in the Gospel of Luke* (Collegeville, MN: Liturgical Press, 1996); Turid Karlsen Seim, *The Double Message: Patterns of Gender in Luke-Acts* (Nashville: Abingdon Press, 1994); Jane D. Schaberg and Sharon H. Ringe, "Luke," in *Women's Bible Commentary*, ed. Carol A. Newsom, Sharon H. Ringe, and Jacqueline E. Lapsley, 3d rev. ed. (Louisville: Westminster John Knox, 2012), 493-511.

FOR FURTHER READING

Athans, Mary Christine. *In Quest of the Jewish Mary: The Mother of Jesus in History, Theology, and Spirituality.* Maryknoll, NY: Orbis Books, 2013.

Brown, Raymond E. *Mary in the New Testament: A Collaborative Assessment by Protestant and Roman Catholic Scholars.* Philadelphia: Fortress Press, 1978.

Johnson, Elizabeth A. *Truly Our Sister: A Thology of Mary in the Communion of Saints.* New York: Continuum, 2003.

———. *Dangerous Memories: A Mosaic of Mary in Scripture; Drawn from "Truly Our Sister."* New York: Continuum, 2004.

Levine, Amy-Jill, with Maria Mayo Robbins. *A Feminist Companion to Mariology.* FCNT 10. London: T&T Clark, 2005.

Wilson, Brittany E. "Mary and Her Interpreters." Pages 511–16 in *Women's Bible Commentary,* 3d ed. Edited by Carol Newsom, Sharon H. Ringe, and Jacqueline Lapsley. Louisville: Westminster John Knox, 2012.

CHAPTER 5

Women Healed and Healing

The Gospels include a number of stories of women who are healed by Jesus: Simon's mother-in-law (Mark 1:29-31 // Matt 8:14-17 // Luke 4:38-41); Jairus's daughter and a woman with hemorrhages (Mark 5:21-43 // Matt 9:18-26 // Luke 8:40-56); the daughter of a Canaanite woman (Mark 7:24-30 // Matt 15:21-28);[1] Mary Magdalene, Joanna, Susanna, and many other Galilean women (Luke 8:1-3);[2] and a woman bent double for eighteen years (Luke 13:10-17). Another incident features a woman who is forgiven (Luke 7:36-50). Some of the stories highlight the audacity and persistence of the women in approaching Jesus, as the woman with the hemorrhages and the Canaanite woman. Some emphasize the severity of the illness, which then highlights Jesus' power to overcome it, as with Simon's mother-in-law,[3] the woman with the hemorrhages,[4] Mary Magdalene,[5] and the woman bent double for eighteen years. In some of the stories, the response of the women who are healed is to serve others, such as Simon's mother-in-law, Mary Magdalene, Joanna, Susanna, and the other Galilean women (see below, chap. 6). The woman who stands up straight for the first time

---

1. In the Gospel of Mark she is identified as "a Gentile of Syrophoenician origin" (7:26); Matthew calls her "a Canaanite woman" from the region of Tyre and Sidon (15:21-22).

2. Luke 8:2 says the women "had been cured of evil spirits and infirmities." It does not say explicitly that it was Jesus who did the healing, but implies it.

3. Luke adds "very high" to describe her fever (4:38).

4. She had been suffering for twelve years, a symbolic number for a full amount of time, and she "had endured much under many physicians, and had spent all that she had; and she was no better, but rather grew worse" (Mark 5:25-26).

5. "Seven demons" in Luke 8:2 signifies that she was very ill; seven being the perfect number, and demon possession referring to any number of illnesses.

in eighteen years keeps on giving praise to God, precisely the purpose of sabbath. The woman who has been forgiven makes a lavish demonstration of love toward Jesus, which then provokes criticism by Simon, the host (Luke 7:36-50).

In this chapter, we focus on two of these incidents: the Canaanite woman who pleads for her daughter (Matt 15:21-28) and the woman who shows great love (Luke 7:36-50). In the first we explore the stance of the woman who will not take "no" for an answer. In the second, we examine the way in which the woman who pours out her love is an icon of the Christ.

A Canaanite Woman with Dogged Determination

> [21]Jesus left that place and went away to the district of Tyre and Sidon. [22]Just then a Canaanite woman from that region came out and started shouting, "Have mercy on me, Lord, Son of David; my daughter is tormented by a demon." [23]But he did not answer her at all. And his disciples came and urged him, saying, "Send her away, for she keeps shouting after us." [24]He answered, "I was sent only to the lost sheep of the house of Israel." [25]But she came and knelt before him, saying, "Lord, help me." [26]He answered, "It is not fair to take the children's food and throw it to the dogs." [27]She said, "Yes, Lord, yet even the dogs eat the crumbs that fall from their masters' table." [28]Then Jesus answered her, "Woman, great is your faith! Let it be done for you as you wish." And her daughter was healed instantly. (Matt 15:21-28)

A Foray into Foreign Territory

In the Gospel of Matthew, as also in Mark and Luke, Jesus concentrates his ministry in Galilee, journeying to Jerusalem only one fateful time (Matt 19:1). There is one time, however, when Mark (7:24-30) and Matthew (15:21-28) recount an instance in which Jesus goes out to the Mediterranean coast, to the region of Tyre and Sidon. The evangelist does not tell us why Jesus went there. The Matthean Jesus is intent on ministering only to the lost sheep of the house of Israel (Matt 10:6), which leaves us puzzled as to why he leaves his base territory in Galilee to go toward the region of

Tyre and Sidon. It may be that Jesus has gone there to rest and to lay low, for in the previous chapter Matthew recounts how Herod has executed John the Baptist, Jesus' predecessor (14:3–12). Ominously, the story of the death of John is preceded by the notice that Jesus has also come to Herod's attention. This sounds the death knell for Jesus, as Herod remarks that Jesus is John the Baptist raised from the dead (14:1–2). Perhaps, then, the reason that Jesus goes toward Tyre and Sidon is that there he would be out of Herod's jurisdiction. In addition, it is a big city, where he can be anonymous. He needs time to grieve over his beloved predecessor. He needs to regroup and strategize how best to carry on the mission without having it cut short in an untimely fashion. He needs to discern when the propitious moment is to speak out, to heal, and to continue gathering in the "lost sheep of the house of Israel."

A Plea for Mercy

But Jesus is recognized. A Canaanite woman comes up to him pleading, "Have mercy on me, Lord, Son of David; my daughter is tormented by a demon" (15:22). By labeling the woman with the outmoded term "Canaanite," Matthew makes her the archetypal enemy, those with whom Israel struggled for possession of the land. Oddly, this so-called enemy knows both the right Jewish prayer formulas and the proper messianic title for Jesus. Her impassioned plea, *Eleēson me, kyrie*, "Lord, have mercy," sounds just like the lament in Psalm 109:26, and just like the pleas of the blind men (Matt 9:27; 20:30–31) and of the father of the boy with epilepsy (Matt 17:15), who also call out to Jesus for mercy, as Son of David. In those instances, he quickly heals them. To this woman he says nothing. No response whatsoever. Never has Jesus turned away anyone who pleaded with him for compassion. Moreover, Jesus' disciples encourage him, "Send her away, for she keeps shouting after us" (Matt 15:23). He finally deigns to speak with her, insisting he has nothing for her: "I was sent only to the lost sheep of the house of Israel" (15:24).

Perhaps if the woman were seeking healing for herself, she might have given up more quickly, but it is her daughter who is sick. There is nothing that fires up a mother's audacity more than her desire for her child's well-being. She kneels before Jesus, a gesture one makes toward the holy, but in so doing, she also blocks his way, forcing him to act on her behalf. She pleads again, "Lord, help me" (15:25).

Refusing to Return Insult for Insult

This time Jesus' response is outrageously insulting: "It is not fair to take the children's food and throw it to the dogs" (15:26). Some biblical scholars and preachers want to tone down the ugliness of this exchange. They try to pretty it up and make Jesus' remark into an endearing comment aimed at a pet. Others think Jesus is reciting a common saying of his day that reflected the animosity that Galileans had toward the people on the coast. There is no evidence for such a saying, but we know from several references in the Bible that Galilee was the breadbasket for the city folk in Tyre and Sidon. In 1 Kings 5:10-11 we read of how Hiram, king of Tyre, sent Solomon cedar wood to build his temple. In exchange, Solomon sent food to Hiram. There is also a reference in Acts 12:20 to Tyre and Sidon's dependence on Herod's territory for food. It may have been that when there were shortages, the food still got exported to the coastal cities, leaving the Galileans bitterly resentful toward the Romans. But no matter how one understands the genesis of Jesus' comment, calling the woman a dog is a gross insult.

Rather than turn away in anger, or return insult for insult, the mother redirects her hurt, finding clever words, and remaining respectful toward Jesus, "Yes, Lord, yet even the dogs eat the crumbs that fall from their masters' table" (15:28). With that, something shifts in Jesus. He recognizes that she is right, his vision has been too narrow. She stretches him to see her not as "other" or as "enemy" but as one of his own, one with whom he shares a common humanity, a common faith in God, a common desire for the well-being of all children. He recognizes her great faith, a significant moment in this gospel, when the Matthean Jesus so often chides his disciples for their "little faith" (Matt 6:30; 8:26; 14:31; 16:8; 17:20).

In the Sermon on the Mount, Jesus had taught his disciples not to return insult for insult, and not to allow anyone to be treated as an enemy (Matt 5:38-48). He had given them three examples of how to respond to insults and humiliation in ways that can break cycles of violence by finding a way to respond to an aggressor without using their violent tactics.[6] Now this "enemy" mirrors back to him his very own teaching!

---

6. See further Walter Wink, *Engaging the Powers: Discernment and Resistance in a World of Domination* (Minneapolis: Fortress, 1992), 175-86.

Women Who Answer Back

In many cultures, women are socialized never to answer back to men in authority. In this story the woman's retort is an expression of laudable faith and is a vehicle for speaking truth and for bringing about the healing of a suffering little girl. It also opens up a transformative moment for Jesus himself. Jesus' initial responses to the woman do not paint him in a very good light: he first ignores her, then insults her. We can find ourselves trying to skirt around this exchange, as many commentators do, or we may want to explain that Jesus didn't really mean it the way it sounds. When we stand with the woman in the story and let ourselves hear it from her perspective, there's no denying the ugliness of his words. If Jesus was indeed fully human in all things but sin (Heb 4:15) and grew in wisdom and grace (Luke 2:52), then it is altogether plausible that encounters with women such as this one helped him comprehend more fully the mission God had entrusted to him.

In contrast to Luke, who depicts Jesus as reaching out to Gentiles, Matthew portrays him intent on leading his own people to a renewed sense of faithfulness to God and not actively reaching out to people outside his own. As Matthew tells it, encounters such as this one spark in Jesus the idea that his mission is for all people, a notion that will be fanned into flame by those who carry on his mission after his death (Matt 28:19).

Crumbs That Fall from the Table

The Canaanite woman's retort also opens up important questions about eating, feeding, and nourishing, with regard to both physical and spiritual hunger. This episode is surrounded by two stories of Jesus feeding multitudes of hungry people (Matt 14:15–21 and 15:29–39). Jesus' compassion for his own people in their need (14:14; 15:32) prompts him to give them satisfying food. Yet the cries for mercy from an outsider at first go unheeded. In a world in which some are overfed while others are starving, the Canaanite woman's plea can help those who have more than enough to eat to hear the cries of their needy brothers and sisters and to respond not only in mercy, but in work toward changing systems for more just distribution of food globally. It is not enough for hungry ones to get the scraps that fall from the table of the satiated, for in God's design, all are to enjoy "a feast of rich food" and of "well-aged wines" (Isa 25:6).

More often than not, it is women who are in charge of feeding multitudes—at family gatherings or in parish potlucks, for example. In situations of extreme need, as in Peru, during the terrorizing time of the Sendero Luminoso (Shining Path) in the 1980s, it was mothers who organized *comedores populares* (communal kitchens) to feed masses of people, even when they were threatened with death for doing so. Like the Canaanite woman, the godly actions of women who see that all are fed and satisfied can lead the way to global practices of just distribution of food. The plea of the Canaanite woman, "Lord, have mercy," is also a liturgical formula, leading us to the reflect on inclusiveness at the eucharistic table. Not only is it a reminder of the struggles in early Christian communities over Gentile inclusion, but it confronts us with questions about full inclusion of women in the liturgical and theological life of contemporary Christian communities. Rather than be content with "scraps" of leftover auxiliary jobs, the Canaanite woman might help women insist that all deserve to be more fully fed by hearing female voices as well as male interpret the Scriptures in the preached word, and by receiving the blessed and broken bread from female hands as well as male.

A Woman Who Loves Lavishly

[36]One of the Pharisees asked Jesus to eat with him, and he went into the Pharisee's house and took his place at the table. [37]And a woman in the city, who was a sinner, having learned that he was eating in the Pharisee's house, brought an alabaster jar of ointment. [38]She stood behind him at his feet, weeping, and began to bathe his feet with her tears and to dry them with her hair. Then she continued kissing his feet and anointing them with the ointment. [39]Now when the Pharisee who had invited him saw it, he said to himself, "If this man were a prophet, he would have known who and what sort of woman this is who is touching him—that she is a sinner." [40]Jesus spoke up and said to him, "Simon, I have something to say to you." "Teacher," he replied, "speak." [41]"A certain creditor had two debtors; one owed five hundred denarii, and the other fifty. [42]When they could not pay, he canceled the debts for both of them. Now which of them will love him more?" [43]Simon answered, "I suppose the one for whom he canceled the greater debt." And Jesus said to him, "You have judged rightly." [44]Then turning toward the woman, he said to Simon, "Do

you see this woman? I entered your house; you gave me no water for my feet, but she has bathed my feet with her tears and dried them with her hair. [45]You gave me no kiss, but from the time I came in she has not stopped kissing my feet. [46]You did not anoint my head with oil, but she has anointed my feet with ointment. [47]Therefore, I tell you, her sins, which were many, have been forgiven; hence she has shown great love. But the one to whom little is forgiven, loves little." [48]Then he said to her, "Your sins are forgiven." [49]But those who were at the table with him began to say among themselves, "Who is this who even forgives sins?" [50]And he said to the woman, "Your faith has saved you; go in peace." (Luke 7:36-50)

Various Versions

In each of the four gospels there is a story of a woman who anoints Jesus, but in the other three accounts, the anointing takes place at the start of the passion narrative (Mark 14:3-9; Matt 26:6-13; John 12:1-8), whereas the Lucan version is situated in the middle of the Galilean ministry.[7] In Mark and Matthew, the woman is nameless and anoints Jesus' head, a prophetic gesture like that of Samuel as he anointed Saul (1 Sam 10:1) and later David (1 Sam 16:13) as king. In the Gospel of John, Mary of Bethany anoints Jesus' feet, which Jesus interprets as preparation for his burial (12:7). There are many similar details in the four accounts. It is likely that there were originally two strands of tradition: one that told of a woman anointing Jesus before his death, and another recounting an incident where a woman wept over Jesus' feet and anointed them, with details passing from one to the other in the retelling.

In Luke's version, the focus is on the identity of Jesus as prophet, a theme that is very strong throughout the Third Gospel. The incident is situated on the heels of a discussion about how people see what they want to see and don't always perceive correctly. Or if they do perceive correctly, they reject what God is doing through the prophetic messengers they are sent. The episode at the home of Simon zeros in on the two very divergent perceptions by Jesus and his host. With a zinger of a parable, Jesus confronts Simon

---

7. For more detail, see chap. 8 of my book *Choosing the Better Part? Women in the Gospel of Luke* (Collegeville, MN: Liturgical Press, 1996).

about what he sees and invites him to see differently. How Simon sees the anointing woman is intimately connected to how he perceives Jesus.

The episode begins with a description of the woman and what she did (vv. 36-38). Then follow the two divergent interpretations of her actions by Simon and Jesus. Simon sees her as a sinner and is convinced that Jesus is no prophet if he doesn't perceive her this way too. Jesus responds with a little parable about two debtors, and Simon easily gets the point. But can Simon get the point in the real-life situation? Jesus turns back to the woman and asks Simon pointedly, "Do you see this woman?" (v. 44). Jesus then recounts what he sees: his feet bathed with her tears, dried with her hair, and covered with ceaseless kisses and precious ointment. He sees her lavish gestures of love poured out toward him in response to her having been forgiven much. What he sees of Simon is that he offered no water for his feet, no kiss, no anointing, and little, if any, love. The whole episode is an open-ended parable, and we don't know what Simon's response is. As much as we might not find Simon an appealing character, it may be good to stand with him and hear the challenge from Jesus about how we see and what misperceptions we may have that need to be healed.

Look Again

Because of the ways we have heard this text explained and preached, we are conditioned to see the woman as Simon does, and we may miss its impact. First, the text indicates that the woman has already been forgiven before she comes in to the banquet. How and when and by whom? The text does not give us that part of the story. That it was Jesus who forgave her is implied in the grumbling of Simon's table companions about him (v. 49) and in the fact that her loving ministrations are directed toward him. That the forgiveness took place before the dinner is indicated in v. 37, where the tense of the verb *ēn,* "was," is imperfect, which has the connotation "used to be"; she is no longer the sinner she was in the past. In addition, the verb *apheontai,* "have been forgiven" (v. 47), is in the perfect tense, which expresses an action in the past whose effects endure into the present. Moreover, Jesus' parable and his interpretation of the woman's actions indicate that forgiveness comes first,[8] then her outpouring of love. Again in

8. Some translations of v. 47 render the conjunction *hoti* as "because" rather than "therefore." Both meanings are possible, but the context and the point of the parable in vv. 41-42

v. 48, using the perfect tense of the verb *apheōntai,* "have been forgiven," Jesus reaffirms to the woman that her sins have been forgiven in their past encounter. Jesus' challenge to Simon is to see her as a person who has been forgiven much and who consequently loves greatly, not as one who has sinned much.

Titles

One of the things to notice is that most Bible translators keep us seeing the woman the way Simon does, not the way Jesus does, by the titles they append to this passage. There are no titles in the Greek text; translators have added them to make it easier for us to find our place. Notice how translations emphasize the sinfulness of the woman: "The Pardon of a Sinful Woman" (NAB), "The Woman Who Was a Sinner" (NJB, NRSV), and "A Sinful Woman Forgiven" (Harper Collins Study Bible). La Nueva Biblia Latinoamericana confuses matters entirely by making her "La mujer pecadora de Magdala" (The sinful woman from Magdala[!]). None points the reader to the way Jesus perceives her by entitling it, "A Woman Who Shows Great Love."

What Kinds of Sins?

Another common thread in commentaries is speculation about the kinds of sins the woman committed. By contrast, very few if any ask that question about Peter, whose response to Jesus' call is, "Go away from me, Lord, for I am a sinful man!" (Luke 5:8). One might wonder if this is not revealing some sexism when the question is asked about the woman but not about Peter. A skewed understanding of Genesis 3 contributes to perpetuating the notion that women are always the instigators of sinfulness.

Most people are pretty sure they know what kind of sinner the woman in Luke 7:37 was—a prostitute. Although the text does not say what kind of sins she committed, readers think they can tell from her actions. They point

---

clearly indicate that here the meaning is "therefore"—the woman is forgiven, therefore she demonstrates great love. Here, as everywhere else in the Bible, God's forgiveness is offered freely and undeservedly. It is not something we can earn by acts of love.

to her being known in the city as a sinner, her loose hair, her expensive flask of perfume, her very presence at the banquet, and the way she touches Jesus as indications that she was in the sex trade. Each of these details could have another meaning, if we look from another angle.

Known to Be a Sinner   That Simon knows the woman to be a sinner does not indicate that she was a prostitute, although we might chuckle over one student's quip that the reason Simon knew her was that he had been a client of hers! If the woman were ill or disabled, that might have caused her to be considered a sinner. Whatever her offense, it was something that was known in the community, but Luke has not told us what it was.

Loose Hair, Loose Woman?   Some commentators think the woman's loose hair is a tell-tale sign that she is a prostitute. They cite the Tosefta and the Talmud (e.g., t. Sotah 5.9; y. Gittin 9.50d), where it says that a married Jewish woman was not to let down her hair in the presence of other men. But these rabbinic texts are considerably later than Jesus' time and that of the gospel writers, and the customs described therein may not have any relevance to the first century. In the Song of Songs, a text that likely dates to the end of the Babylonian exile (538 BCE), the bridegroom-to-be is extolling the beauties of his beloved and says her long, dark, flowing hair is "like a flock of goats, moving down the slopes of Gilead" (Song 4:1; 6:5). Likewise, Jesus perceives the woman who dries his feet with her loosened hair as loving and beloved.

The Alabaster Jar   Some scholars point to the alabaster jar as a sure indication that the woman is a prostitute. Kenneth Bailey, for example, notes that prostitutes would wear a flask with perfume around the neck that hung down below the breast, used to sweeten the breath and perfume the person.[9] Some interpreters reason that the very expensive flask and ointment could be purchased only by a woman who made her living in the sex trade.

There are three flaws in this reasoning. First, the alabaster jar and ointment indicate that the woman had access to something expensive, but we do not know the source of it. Second, we have no evidence that prostitutes were accustomed to wearing flasks of perfume around their necks. Third, women earned money in many different occupations: weav-

---

9. Kenneth E. Bailey, *Poet and Peasant and Through Peasant Eyes*, 2 vols. in 1 (Grand Rapids: Eerdmans, 1983), 2.8.

ers, midwives, doctors, hairdressers, wet nurses, masseuses, attendants, musicians, dyers and dealers (like Lydia in Acts 16:14), and leather workers (like Prisca with her husband, Aquila, in Acts 18:3).[10] It is not only a modern phenomenon that women work in many kinds of occupations outside the home. In addition, from at least fifth century BCE (when the book of Numbers reached its final form), unmarried women who had no brothers could inherit money and property from their fathers (Num 27:8). Closer to the time of Jesus, there is evidence from a collection of documents found near the Dead Sea in 1960 which date to the early second century CE, that an upper-middle class Jewish woman, Babatha, had money and goods and control over them.

Women at Banquets Some interpreters argue that only a prostitute would attend a banquet with men. It is true that there were courtesans who were invited to banquets to enhance the pleasure of the male guests. But in the Roman period, respectable women were beginning to attend banquets with men. The woman who comes to Simon's house, however, is not participating in the banquet.[11] Nor does she do any of the things that banquet courtesans were known to do: engage in witty conversation or discussion with the banqueters, drink with them, recline beside them, dance, act, play the flute or harp, or in any way entertain.[12] Nor is she named by any of the known terms for such women: *pornē* ("prostitute, whore"), *koinē* ("common," i.e., "shared by all"), or *hetaira* ("companion to men," the term for the highest-class prostitutes).

Touching Jesus' Feet Finally, for some commentators, the way in which the woman kisses and touches Jesus' feet is proof positive that she is a prostitute. Only such a woman would have the audacity to touch Jesus in this way,

---

10. See Jane Gardner, *Women in Roman Law and Society* (Bloomington: Indiana University Press, 1986), 233–55.

11. How the woman got into Simon's house if she was not an invited guest is explained by the practice of virtuous Jews opening their houses to the needy, particularly for Sabbath eve supper. This custom is mentioned in several rabbinic texts: *m. Avot* 1:5; *t. Berakhot* 4:8; *Ta'an.* 20.b. See further John Koenig, *New Testament Hospitality*, OBT 17 (Philadelphia: Fortress, 1985).

12. See descriptions of banquet courtesans in Kathleen E. Corley, *Private Women, Public Meals: Social Conflict in the Synoptic Tradition* (Peabody, MA: Hendrickson, 1993), 38–48; see also Sarah Pomeroy, *Goddesses, Whores, Wives, and Slaves: Women in Classical Antiquity* (New York: Dorset, 1975), 88–92.

they reason. However, a number of texts in Greco-Roman literature show that kissing the feet was a sign of deep reverence.[13] It is curious, moreover, that no one ever interprets Jesus' actions this way when he washes and lovingly touches the feet of his disciples at the Last Supper (John 13:1–20).

An Icon of Christ

What if we were to shift our perspective and see the woman the way Jesus saw her? There is more than a forgiven sinner. Her copious tears of joy as she ministers to Jesus contrast with those of Peter, who weeps bitterly after he abandons the ministry and denies Jesus (Luke 22:62). Her ceaseless kisses stand in contrast to the betraying kiss of Judas (Luke 22:47). Her position at Jesus' feet is that of a servant,[14] the position that Jesus himself embraces (Luke 22:26–27). Her loving action of breaking the alabaster flask and pouring out its precious contents is a symbolic emulation of Christ, who allows his body to be broken and his precious blood poured out for all his beloved (Luke 22:20). She is an icon of Christ! For many Christians, it is still difficult to see women as fully able to be an image of Christ and to act *in persona Christi*. Just as Simon's inability to perceive the woman correctly inhibited his ability to see Jesus as God's prophet, so our ability to more fully perceive Christ in our midst is linked to our ability to see him embodied in his female followers.

Women Healers

In the Gospel accounts of women healed and forgiven by Jesus, they are objects of Jesus' compassion, rather than subjects actively engaged in procuring their own well-being and that of others. The story of the Canaanite woman is an exception. In the episode with the forgiven woman in Luke 7:36–50, for example, she is the object of discussion, but not an interlocutor with the men. And while women are recipients of healing and forgiveness in the Gospels and Acts, there are no episodes in which they appear as

13. Xenophon *Cyr.* 7.5.32; Polybius 15.1.7; Aritophanes *Vesp.* 608.

14. Images that have the woman crawling under the table like a dog are mistaken. Banqueters reclined, with their feet extended behind them, which would have been easy for the woman to reach. Note that the verb *kateklithē*, "took his place," in 7:36 literally means "reclined."

agents of healing or forgiveness. Jesus commissions his disciples to heal the sick, cure diseases, cast out unclean spirits, and raise the dead (Matt 10:8; Mark 6:7; Luke 9:1-6; 10:9),[15] as he himself does, and commissions them to proclaim repentance for forgiveness of sins in his name to all nations, beginning from Jerusalem (24:47). But only male disciples, primarily Peter and Paul, are shown to do so.[16] In some ways, this mirrors the contemporary situation where, in many places, the medical profession is dominated by males. But in numerous traditional cultures all over the world, it is the women who have been recognized for centuries as being particularly skilled in the healing arts.[17] In the state of Chiapas in southern Mexico, for example, indigenous women work collectively to preserve their knowledge of local herbs and their role and art as healers, which they have exercised in their communities for tens of thousands of years.[18]

Although their stories may not be preserved in the Gospels, we can surmise that the women who had experienced healing and forgiveness from Jesus would themselves have become conduits of well-being for others.

FOR DISCUSSION

1. What do you hear in the story of the Canaanite mother when you look at it from her perspective?
2. In what way does the Canaanite woman invite you to go beyond being satisfied with "crumbs from the table"?
3. How does perceiving women as icons of Christ enable us to perceive Jesus more fully?

15. When Jesus appoints a further seventy to go out in pairs to cure the sick and proclaim the nearness of the kingdom (Luke 10:1-12), this symbolic full number can be interpreted as including women as well as men disciples.

16. See Acts 3:1-10; 5:12-16; 8:7; 9:32-35; 14:8-10; 16:18; 19:12; 28:8-9 for stories of healings, resuscitations, and exorcisms. See Acts 2:38; 5:31; 8:22; 10:43; 13:38; 26:18, where it is primarily Peter and Paul who proclaim repentance and forgiveness.

17. See, for example, Max Dashú, "Woman Shamans," www.suppressedhistories.net/articles/womanshaman.html.

18. During the conflicts between the Zapatistas and the Mexican government in the 1990s, many women refused to flee their homes and convinced their husbands to remain also, partly because the women knew all the medicinal qualities of the local plants and herbs. They argued, What would they do in a strange land without these? See Ligia Valdivieso Eguiguren, "Género y medicina natural y andina," *Alpanchis* 57 (2001): 235-39. See also "The Healer" in Chiapas Media Project, www.chiapasmediaproject.org/healer.

FOR FURTHER READING

Humphries-Brooks, Stephenson. "The Canaanite Women in Matthew." Pages 138–57 in *A Feminist Companion to Matthew*. Edited by Amy-Jill Levine, with Marianne Blickenstaff. FCNT 1. Sheffield: Sheffield Academic Press, 2001.

Levine, Amy-Jill. "Matthew's Advice to a Divided Readership." Pages 22–41 in *The Gospel of Matthew in Current Study*. Edited by David E. Aune. Grand Rapids: Eerdmans, 2001.

O'Day, Gail R. "Surprised by Faith." Pages 114–25 in *A Feminist Companion to Matthew*. Edited by Amy-Jill Levine, with Marianne Blickenstaff. FCNT 1. Sheffield: Sheffield Academic Press, 2001.

Reid, Barbara. *Choosing the Better Part? Women in the Gospel of Luke*. Collegeville, MN: Liturgical Press, 1996, 107–23.

Wainwright, Elaine M. "Not without My Daughter: Gender and Demon Possession in Matthew 15:21–28." Pages 126–37 in *A Feminist Companion to Matthew*. Edited by Amy-Jill Levine, with Marianne Blickenstaff. FCNT 1. Sheffield: Sheffield Academic Press, 2001.

———. *Women Healing/Healing Women: The Genderization of Healing in Early Christianity*. London: Equinox, 2006.

CHAPTER 6

Deacon Phoebe and Other Women Ministers

In many Christian churches, the debate continues whether women today may be ordained to the diaconate. Some denominations have resolved the question affirmatively and do have women deacons. Others have responded with a firm No! Still others continue to study the issue. There is no question that there is firm basis in Scripture and tradition for female deacons. In this chapter, we explore some of the ministries of women in the Pauline churches, starting with deacon Phoebe (Rom 16:1-2).

Phoebe, Deacon and Leader

> [1]I commend to you our sister Phoebe, a deacon of the church at Cenchreae; [2]so that you may welcome her in the Lord as is fitting for the saints, and help her in whatever way she may require from you, for she has been a benefactor of many and of myself as well. (Rom 16:1-2)

The last chapter of Paul's letter to the Romans opens with a strong commendation of Phoebe. There is some debate whether Romans 16 was a separate letter destined for Ephesus, added later to the letter sent to Rome. Whatever the original destination, it is clear that Paul is endorsing the ministry of Phoebe, who was deacon of the church in Cenchreae, one of the two ports for the bustling city of Corinth. Situated just south of the isthmus that connects the Peloponnesian peninsula to mainland Greece, Corinth had many merchants and travelers passing through, which provided much opportunity for evangelization. The Acts of the Apostles (18:11) notes that

Paul spent eighteen months in Corinth. From Paul's own letters, we know that he made at least one more trip there and that this was one of his most beloved, also most challenging, communities. Paul's esteem for Phoebe comes through strongly in the two short verses in which he commends her to the community in Rome. It is likely that she is the carrier of the letter, and she may have been the one who read it aloud to the various house churches in Rome. Paul may even have discussed its contents with her so that she could respond to any questions that arose from it.[1]

It is notable that Phoebe is the only person in the New Testament who is named with a ministerial title. Although some translations render her title "deaconess," in fact, the Greek noun *diakonos* is both masculine and feminine; there is no basis for making a distinction in English between "deacon" and "deaconess." It is important to remember that ordination rituals did not yet exist, and the ministerial roles in Paul's days were still quite fluid. There were no job descriptions for deacons. Instead, what the New Testament gives us are the qualifications that make for a good minister.

Qualifications for Ministers

In the first letter to Timothy we find a list of desired qualities, first for *episkopoi* (literally, "overseers," later translated "bishops"), then for deacons:

> [8]Deacons likewise must be serious, not double-tongued, not indulging in much wine, not greedy for money; [9]they must hold fast to the mystery of the faith with a clear conscience. [10]And let them first be tested; then, if they prove themselves blameless, let them serve as deacons. [11]Women likewise must be serious, not slanderers, but temperate, faithful in all things. [12]Let deacons be married only once, and let them manage their children and their households well; [13]for those who serve well as deacons gain a good standing for themselves and great boldness in the faith that is in Christ Jesus. (1 Tim 3:8-13)

It is interesting that the qualities desired in Christian ministers are those of a good household manager (v. 12) and are similar to the charac-

---

1. Beverly Roberts Gaventa, "Romans," in *Women's Bible Commentary*, 3d ed., ed. Carol Newsom, Sharon H. Ringe, and Jacqueline Lapsley (Louisville: Westminster John Knox, 2012), 555.

teristics of a good general listed by Onasander, a first-century Greek philosopher, in his work *Strategikos:*

> I believe, then, that we must choose a general, not because of noble birth as priests are chosen, nor because of wealth as the superintendents of the gymnasia, but because he is temperate, self-restrained, vigilant, frugal, hardened to labour, alert, free from avarice, neither too young nor too old, indeed a father of children if possible, a ready speaker, and a man with a good reputation.[2]

Various Kinds of Ministries

To gain insight into what kind of ministry Phoebe would have been engaged in, we can look at other occurrences of *diakonos* in Paul's letters, as well as the uses in the New Testament of the verb *diakonein* ("to minister, to serve") and the noun *diakonia* ("ministry, service"). Twice Paul uses *diakonos* to refer to Jesus as a servant (Rom 15:8; Gal 2:17). In Romans 13:4 ruling authorities are said to be God's servants *(diakonos)*. Paul uses *diakonos* to refer to those in leadership positions in the church: himself (2 Cor 3:6; 6:4; 11:23), also himself with Apollos (1 Cor 3:5) and with Timothy (Phil 1:1).

In the Synoptic Gospels, Jesus uses the verb *diakonein* to describe his ministry: he has come "not to be served [*diakonēthēnai*] but to serve [*diakonēsai*]" (Mark 10:45; Matt 20:28). In the Last Supper scene in Luke's Gospel, Jesus further defines diaconal service as leadership, as he says that the leader must be "like one who serves [*ho diakonōn*]" (Luke 22:26).

Two types of diaconal service are distinguished in Acts 6:1-7: "ministering at table" *(diakonein trapezais,* v. 2) and "ministry of the word" *(diakonia tou logou,* v. 4). This text relates that the Hellenists, that is, the Greek speakers in the community in Jerusalem, complained against the Hebrew speakers that their widows were being neglected in the daily distribution *(diakonia)*. It is not clear what the conflict entailed. Some translators presume that it involved food (NRSV has "daily distribution of food"), but the

---

2. Transcription available online from the 1986 reprint of the Loeb Classical Library volume containing Aeneas Tacticus, and Onasander, Greek text and facing English translation: Harvard University Press, 1928, http://penelope.uchicago.edu/Thayer/E/Roman/Texts/Onasander/A*.html.

text does not specify. Most commentators, picturing widows as needy and dependent, surmise that they were on the receiving end of the ministry. However, many widows in Luke and Acts were doing the ministering,[3] and it may have been the case that they were overlooked by the leaders of the community when the various ministerial assignments were given.[4] The Twelve decide to resolve the issue by appointing seven Hellenist men to the ministry of the table, while the Twelve would devote themselves to prayer and ministry of the word. It is then reported that this proposal "pleased the whole community" (v. 5). One wonders whether the widows themselves were included in the discussion and the decision-making and whether they were as pleased as the men.

It is interesting that this distinction between *diakonia* of the word and *diakonia* of the table does not hold up, as in the very next verses of Acts, Stephen, who was chosen for table ministry, is engaged in eloquent debate (Acts 6:8-15) and then delivers a lengthy speech (7:2-53). Similarly, Philip goes from place to place proclaiming the word (Acts 8:4, 40) and interprets a text from Isaiah for the Ethiopian eunuch (8:26-39). He becomes known as "Philip the evangelist" (Acts 21:8), and no mention is made of his service at table.

Another kind of diaconal ministry is financial, as in Luke 8:3, where Mary Magdalene, Joanna, Susanna, and many other Galilean women "provided for" *(diēkonoun)* Jesus and his disciples "out of their resources" *(ek tōn hyparchontōn autais)*. The imperfect tense of the verb *diēkonoun* implies repeated action in the past, not a one-time donation. The noun *hyparchontōn*, "resources," always refers to possessions, property, money, or goods in Luke and Acts.[5] That the money belongs to the women is indicated by the

---

3. E.g., Anna the prophet (2:36-38); some of the Galilean women in Luke 8:1-3 may have been widows, as was also possible for Martha and Mary (Luke 10:38-42). Dorcas, herself likely a widow, houses other ministering widows (Acts 9:36-43). There is also the story of the widow who contributes her whole livelihood to the temple treasury (Luke 21:1-4 // Mark 12:41-44). See 1 Tim 5:3-16 for the qualifications for those seeking to belong officially to the ministering widows.

4. See further Barbara Reid, "The Power of Widows and How to Suppress It (Acts 6:1-7)," in *A Feminist Companion to the Acts of the Apostles,* ed. Amy-Jill Levine, FCNT 9 (New York: T&T Clark, 2004), 71-88. See also Elisabeth Schüssler Fiorenza, *In Memory of Her: A Feminist Theological Reconstruction of Christian Origins* (New York: Crossroad Publishing, 1984), 165-66, who argues that the conflict involved the role and participation of women at the Eucharistic meal: that the Hellenist widows were not being assigned their turn in the table service or that they were not properly served.

5. See Luke 11:21; 12:15, 33, 44; 14:33; 16:1; 19:8; Acts 4:32.

feminine plural pronoun *autais,* "their." They are not administering the common purse; John 12:6 says this was Judas's job. In two other instances in Acts, *diakonia* has financial connotations, where it refers to the collection for the needy in Jerusalem (Acts 11:29; 12:25).

Finally, *diakonia* also refers to apostolic ministry. The Acts of the Apostles relates that, when it came time to choose a successor for Judas, the community in Jerusalem prayed that they be shown which one was to take his place in the "apostolic ministry" *(diakonias tautēs kai apostolēs),* and Matthias is chosen (Acts 1:25).

After examining the various uses of *diakonos, diakonia,* and *diakonein,* we can surmise that Phoebe could have been engaged in any or all of these diaconal ministries. As leader of the church at Cenchreae, she likely broke open the word for the community by catechizing, preaching, and teaching. She may have presided over the eucharistic table and likely used her financial resources for the support of the community. Serving as ambassador of Paul to Rome, her ministry could also be regarded as apostolic (*apostolos* means "one sent").

Leader of Many

The expression Paul uses in Romans 16:2 confirms that Phoebe was an important leader. He calls her *prostatis* ("leader") of many and of himself as well. The noun *prostatis* is translated variously as "helper" (RSV), "good friend" (NEB), "a great help" (NIV), or "benefactor" (NRSV, NAB). In secular Greek literature *prostatis* is used for "leader" or "ruler" in a political sense. In the Roman period it was used for patrons, those who provided funds and protection and used their political influence for the benefit of those under their patronage. But the translation "patron" in Romans 16:2 would seem to imply that Phoebe only provided funding for the ministry, whereas the context indicates that her role as a leader and administrator was far greater. When Paul acknowledges her leadership of many and of himself as well, this may reflect that, as local leader, she had more influence over the community at Cenchreae than did Paul, who was there only temporarily.[6]

---

6. Sojung Yoon, "Phoebe, a Minister in the Early Christian Church," in *Distant Voices Drawing Near: Essays in Honor of Antoinette Clark Wire,* ed. Holly E. Hearon (Collegeville, MN: Liturgical Press, 2004), 19–31.

Other Ministering Women

While Phoebe is the only person named specifically as *diakonos* in the New Testament, the verb *diakonein* is used of several women in the Synoptic Gospels. In fact, this verb is used *only* with women: Simon's mother-in-law (Mark 1:29-31 // Matt 8:14-17 // Luke 4:38-41), Martha (Luke 10:40), and the group consisting of Mary Magdalene, Joanna, Susanna, and the other Galilean women (Luke 8:3; Mark 15:41 // Matt 27:55 // Luke 23:49). We will explore these stories next, and that of Martha in chapter 8.

Simon's Mother-in-Law

> [14]When Jesus entered Peter's house, he saw his mother-in-law lying in bed with a fever; [15]he touched her hand, and the fever left her, and she got up and began to serve him. (Matt 8:14-15)

All three Synoptic Gospels tell of Simon's mother-in-law, who begins to serve *(diēkonei)* after having been healed by Jesus (Mark 1:29-31; Matt 8:14-17; Luke 4:38-41). While many people envision Simon's mother-in-law serving a meal to Jesus and his disciples, it is likely that the episode also preserves the memory of her service in the Christian mission. When we compare Matthew's version of the story with the call story of Matthew, the tax collector (Matt 9:9-13), we can see a number of similarities. In both stories, Jesus takes the initiative. It is Jesus who calls Matthew as he is walking along and invites Matthew to follow him (Matt 9:9). In Matthew 8:14 it is Jesus who reaches out and touches the hand of Simon's mother-in-law. In Mark's version of the story, Jesus enters the house of Simon and Andrew with James and John, and "they told him about her" (Mark 1:30; likewise Luke 4:38). Another common element to both stories is that, at the beginning of the encounter, Jesus saw *(eiden)* Matthew sitting at the tax booth (Matt 9:9), and he saw *(eiden)* Simon's mother-in-law lying in a bed with a fever (Matt 8:14). Finally, in Matthew's version, Simon's mother-in-law responds to Jesus himself: "She got up and began to serve him" (Matt 8:15). In Mark and Luke's versions, her service is to "them" (Mark 1:31; Luke 4:39). All these similarities between Matthew 8:14-15 and 9:9-13 indicate that, behind the story of the healing of Simon's mother-in-law, there are also traces of the story of her call to discipleship and her memorable service in the Christian community. In its final form as we now have it, it is a healing story. But it may be that, in gatherings of the early followers of Jesus, especially in circles of women, there was more that they talked about than her having been healed.

Mary Magdalene, Joanna, Susanna, and Other Galilean Women

[1]Soon afterwards he went on through cities and villages, proclaiming and bringing the good news of the kingdom of God. The twelve were with him, [2]as well as some women who had been cured of evil spirits and infirmities: Mary, called Magdalene, from whom seven demons had gone out, [3]and Joanna, the wife of Herod's steward Chuza, and Susanna, and many others, who provided for them out of their resources. (Luke 8:1-3)

All four gospels name Mary Magdalene and other Galilean women as followers of Jesus and ministers. In all the Gospels except Luke, they appear only at the end of the story. In the Gospel of Mark, all the other disciples desert Jesus at his arrest (Mark 14:50; similarly Matt 26:56), but the women are there at the crucifixion: "Mary Magdalene, and Mary the mother of James the younger and of Jesus, and Salome" (Mark 15:40).[7] Although Mark has not spoken of them earlier, he notes, "These used to follow him and provided [*diēkonoun*] for him when he was in Galilee; and there were many other women who had come up with him to Jerusalem" (Mark 15:41; similarly Matt 27:55). The imperfect tense of the verbs *ēkolouthoun* ("followed") and *diēkonoun* ("ministered" or "provided") indicate repeated or customary past action. Although the women are not mentioned until the crucifixion scene, the evangelists note that they had been following and ministering all along. After the crucifixion, they see where Jesus is buried (Mark 15:47; Matt 27:61; Luke 23:55) and are the first to go to the tomb and find it empty (Mark 16:1-8; Matt 28:1-12; Luke 24:1-12; John 20:1-18). In the Gospels of Mark and Luke they are commissioned by angelic messengers to tell the good news to the other disciples. In Matthew, Jesus appears to them and commissions

---

7. In Matthew the women are Mary Magdalene, Mary the mother of James and Joseph, and the mother of the sons of Zebedee (27:56). Luke expands the witnesses of the crucifixion to "all his acquaintances, including the women who had followed him from Galilee" (23:49). Only later, in the episode at the empty tomb, does he name them: "Mary Magdalene, Joanna, Mary the mother of James, and the other women with them" (24:10). In the Gospel of John, those standing near the cross are "his mother, and his mother's sister, Mary the wife of Clopas, and Mary Magdalene" (19:25).

them directly; so also in John, where Mary Magdalene is first to see the risen Christ and to be sent to proclaim the good news to the others.

Only Luke tells more of their story earlier in the gospel. In the middle of the Galilean ministry he says that these women who had been healed (see above, chap. 5) were traveling with Jesus through cities and villages, as he was proclaiming the reign of God. He does not say how the women met him or how they were called. We do not know their marital status. It is unusual that Mary of Magdala is identified by the town from which she hails. Most women in the Bible are identified as the daughter, wife, or mother of an important male. It may be that she was a widow, or perhaps never married, though the latter would be unusual in her culture.

One detail that Luke does provide is that many of the women had been healed, presumably by Jesus, and they respond by ministering out of their financial resources, as noted above. The women are not cooking and cleaning and doing the laundry for Jesus and his male disciples. They are bankrolling the mission.

What Luke does not say is where the women's money came from. As noted in chapter 5, women were engaged in many varied kinds of work outside the home. One possibility is that, like Peter, Andrew, James, and John, Mary and some of her companions worked in the fishing industry, since Magdala was an important fishing village, known for its smoked fish. While it was not unusual for women to earn money, it was extraordinary in a male-dominated culture for them to have control over it. That Mary and the other women had the power to determine how their money was spent may indicate that they were widows. One wonders how Joanna managed to give financial support to Jesus when her husband worked for Herod, who was seeking to put an end to him!

Ongoing Legacy of Deacon Phoebe

In all the instances cited above where women are called *diakonos,* are the subject of the verb *diakonein,* and are engaged in *diakonia,* their service is not likely to be cooking and cleaning, as has been traditionally thought. These disciples of Jesus are engaged in various kinds of ministerial service both to and with him and the early communities of his followers. In addition to the New Testament evidence, inscriptions and documents show that women deacons became quite prominent in some segments of the early church, persisting until the twelfth century. A tombstone found on the

Mount of Olives in 1903, which dates to the fourth century, attests to the endurance of Phoebe's legacy: "Here lies the minister and bride of Christ, Sofia the deacon [*diakonos*], the second Phoebe."

Prisca and Other Women Ministers and Leaders

> ³Greet Prisca and Aquila, who work with me in Christ Jesus, ⁴and who risked their necks for my life, to whom not only I give thanks, but also all the churches of the Gentiles. ⁵Greet also the church in their house. (Rom 16:3–5)

Phoebe is not the only woman Paul names with esteem in his letter to the Romans. Following Paul's commendation of her, he sends greetings to a host of others, nine of whom are women. That he mentions them by name indicates their importance in the community. First is Prisca, along with her husband, Aquila, whom he calls "coworkers in Christ Jesus." The term *synergos* ("coworker") is one that Paul uses frequently of those who minister with him. Sometimes he speaks of being coworkers with God (1 Cor 3:9; 1 Thess 3:2), at other times he refers to "my coworkers" (Rom 16:21; 2 Cor 8:23; Phil 2:25; Phlm 24). How Paul and Prisca and Aquila became coworkers Paul does not say. Acts 18 tells of how this Jewish couple had recently come to Corinth from Italy because of Claudius's edict ordering all Jews to leave Rome. Paul sought them out because they shared the same trade: tentmaking and leatherworking. Paul's bonds to Prisca and Aquila deepen during his lengthy, eighteen-month stay in Corinth, and when he leaves, they accompany him to Ephesus (Acts 18:18). There they remain, likely becoming the founders of the Christian community in Ephesus, while Paul continues on to Caesarea. He returns to Ephesus some time later (Acts 19) and spends approximately two and a half years there.

One story about Prisca and Aquila's ministry is recounted in Acts 18:24–27, where they confront an eloquent preacher, Apollos, a Jew from Alexandria. "He had been instructed in the Way of the Lord; and he spoke with burning enthusiasm and taught accurately the things concerning Jesus, though he knew only the baptism of John. He began to speak boldly in the synagogue; but when Priscilla⁸ and Aquila heard him, they took him

---

8. The author of Acts uses the familiar "Priscilla" in 18:2, 18, 26, whereas Paul calls her Prisca (Rom 16:3; 1 Cor 16:19; 2 Tim 4:19).

aside and explained the Way of God to him more accurately" (18:25-26). It is notable that Prisca is named before her husband, both in Acts 18:18, 26 and in Paul's greeting in Romans 16:3 (see also 2 Tim 4:19). This breach of custom may indicate that Prisca was of a higher social status than Aquila or that she was the more influential of the two in the ministry. Paul remarks on how important they are not only to him, but to all the churches of the Gentiles. They are leaders of a house church, which Paul also mentions at the conclusion of his first letter to the Corinthians (1 Cor 16:19).

Female Heads of House Churches

In several other instances in the Pauline letters and in Acts of the Apostles, women are named as leaders of house churches: Nympha (Col 4:15), Lydia (Acts 16:14, 40), and Mary, the mother of John Mark, in Jerusalem (Acts 12:12).[9] As with *diakonos* Phoebe, there is no record of what this ministry entailed or how these women became leaders. They likely had financial resources and ministerial gifts that they placed voluntarily at the service of the community. Or they may have been invited or elected to lead the community. It is not known what their specific jobs were, but they most likely coordinated the care for the community's spiritual and pastoral needs, liturgical celebrations, theological education, and missionary outreach.[10]

Other Women Coworkers

In addition to Prisca, Paul greets four other female coworkers in Romans 16: Mary (v. 6), Tryphaena, Tryphosa, and Persis (v. 12). In these instances, Paul uses the term *kopiōsas* ("laborers," v. 12) and the verb *ekopiasen* ("worked," vv. 6, 12), rather than *synergos* ("coworker"). Paul uses this same verb to speak of his own intense apostolic work (1 Cor 15:10; Gal 4:11). Nothing more is known of these women or their ministries, only that Mary is especially hardworking (v. 6), as is beloved Persis (v. 12). As coworkers and laborers, they no doubt held positions of authority in the community,

9. Although they are not so named, it is possible that Chloe (1 Cor 1:11) and Martha, who "welcomed him [Jesus] into her home" (Luke 10:38), were also heads of house churches.

10. See further Carolyn Osiek, "Women in House Churches," in *Common Life in the Early Church: Essays Honoring Graydon F. Snyder,* ed. Julian V. Hills et al. (Harrisburg, PA: Trinity Press International, 1998), 300-315.

since Paul urged the Corinthians to "be subject to every coworker and laborer [*synergounti kai kopiōnti*]" (1 Cor 16:16).[11]

Two other coworkers named in another of Paul's letters are Euodia and Syntyche, who Paul says "have struggled [*synēthlēsan*] beside me in the work of the gospel, together with Clement and the rest of my co-workers [*synergōn*], whose names are in the book of life" (Phil 4:3). Paul urges them "to be of the same mind in the Lord" (v. 2). With the verb *synathleō* ("to struggle along with someone"), Paul likens the tremendous efforts of these women in the work of the gospel to the exertion of an athlete who strains every muscle in a contest. He counts them among his coworkers who have been working at his side. They may have been a missionary team, like Paul and Barnabas (Acts 13:2), Prisca and Aquila (Acts 16:3), or Andronicus and Junia (Rom 16:7). If this is the case, Paul urges them not to let their dispute end their partnership, as did his own collaboration with Barnabas after their disagreement over John Mark (Acts 15:36–40). Alternatively, Euodia and Syntyche may have been leaders of separate house churches in Philippi. Their conflict may have involved differences of opinion about a theological matter or a liturgical or pastoral practice. Whatever the case, one thing is clear: they are prominent leaders, and their dispute has affected the whole community. Paul speaks about it in a letter that will be read to all, in the hopes that there can be a speedy resolution.

Women Central to the Mission

The evidence in the New Testament and early Christian tradition shows the rich and varied ministries of women in the church from the earliest days. Women were among Jesus' first disciples, accompanied him in mission, and ministered to and with him and continued to do so after his death and resurrection. They placed their finances at the disposal of the mission and served in various other diaconal ministries. Women were not at the margins, nor did they fill in only when there were no men available. While the New Testament provides only a few of their names and stories, these are like the tip of an iceberg. There were many more women deacons than Phoebe, and many more coworkers and ministers than those named in the

11. Author's translation. The verb *hypotassēsthe* is more correctly rendered "be subject to" or "be subordinate to" (NAB) rather than the NRSV translation "put yourselves at the service of."

New Testament. Women have never stopped being central to the Christian mission and ministry.

FOR DISCUSSION

1. What is your experience of women in ministry?
2. What does the New Testament evidence for women ministers say to you?
3. What role does culture play in determining how women serve?

FOR FURTHER READING

Campbell, Joan C. *Phoebe: Patron and Emissary.* Paul's Social Network. Collegeville, MN: Liturgical Press, 2009.

Eisen, Ute. *Women Officeholders in Early Christianity: Epigraphical and Literary Studies.* Collegeville, MN: Liturgical Press, 2000.

Keller, Marie Noël, *Priscilla and Aquila: Paul's Coworkers in Christ Jesus.* Paul's Social Network. Collegeville, MN: Liturgical Press, 2010.

Macy, Gary. *The Hidden History of Women's Ordination: Female Clergy in the Medieval West.* Oxford: Oxford University Press, 2008.

Madigan, Kevin, and Carolyn Osiek. *Ordained Women in the Early Church: A Documentary History.* Baltimore: Johns Hopkins University Press, 2005.

Zagano, Phyllis. *Holy Saturday: An Argument for the Restoration of the Female Diaconate in the Catholic Church.* New York: Crossroad, 2000.

CHAPTER 7

Mary Magdalene, Junia, and Other Apostles

New Testament Apostles

When you ask most Christians to name the apostles, they usually try to recall the list of the Twelve. They begin reciting, "Peter, James, John, Andrew. . . ." It gets harder to remember the ones in the middle. Everybody finishes with ". . . and Judas, who betrayed him." One of the reasons why it gets murky in the middle is that there are four lists of the names of the Twelve in the New Testament, and they do not entirely agree.[1] However, the Twelve are not the only ones who are called apostles in the New Testament. Paul repeatedly calls himself an apostle,[2] as well as others of his coworkers: Apollos (1 Cor 4:6, 9), Barnabas (1 Cor 9:5-6),[3] Epaphroditus (Phil 2:25), Sylvanus and Timothy (1 Thess 1:1 with 2:7), James (Gal 1:19), and Andronicus and Junia (Rom 16:7). This last apostle is a woman. We will return to her shortly. In addition to those explicitly named apostles, a number of women are portrayed as engaging in the work of an apostle: the Samaritan woman (John 4:4-42) and Mary Magdalene (John 20:1-18).

Called by Jesus

Several texts help us understand how one becomes an apostle and what distinguishes apostolic ministry from other kinds of *diakonia*. In the Gos-

---

1. Compare Mark 3:16-19, Matt 10:2-4, Luke 6:14-16, and Acts 1:13.

2. Rom 1:1; 11:13; 1 Cor 1:1; 9:1, 2; 15:9; 2 Cor 1:1; 12:12; Gal 1:1; Eph 1:1; Col 1:1; 1 Tim 1:1; 2:7; 2 Tim 1:1, 11; Titus 1:1.

3. See also Acts 14:4, 14.

91

pel of Mark, it happens this way: Jesus "called to him those he wanted, and they came to him. And he appointed twelve, whom he also named apostles, to be with him, and to be sent out to proclaim the message, and to have authority to cast out demons" (Mark 3:13-15; similarly Luke 6:12-16). He later sends them out two by two with authority over unclean spirits, instructing them "to take nothing for their journey. . . . So they went out and proclaimed that all should repent. They cast out many demons, and anointed with oil many who were sick and cured them" (Mark 6:8, 12-13; similarly Matt 10:1-15; Luke 9:1-6; 10:1-12).

In these texts, the characteristics of an apostle are that the person is chosen and called by Jesus to be with him and then is sent out (*apostolos* means "one sent") to preach, heal, and exorcise demons. It is notable, however, that the Twelve are not the only ones who are called by Jesus and who follow him. Levi, in a story very similar to that of Simon, Andrew, James, and John (Mark 1:16-20), is also called by Jesus, and he leaves everything and follows him (Mark 2:13-14), as did the first four. Others who follow Jesus are Bartimaeus (Mark 10:52), as well as large crowds of people (Mark 2:15; 3:7; 5:24; 8:34; 11:9). Mary Magdalene, Mary the mother of James the younger and of Joses, and Salome followed Jesus both in Galilee and all the way to Jesus' crucifixion in Jerusalem (Mark 15:40-41; similarly Matt 27:55-56; Luke 23:49). Although the Gospels do not recount the story of their call, that Jesus did call these women can be surmised from their response of following and ministering.

Preaching, Healing, Exorcising Demons

The mission that Jesus entrusted to the Twelve was proclamation of the message, casting out demons, and curing diseases and sicknesses (Mark 3:13-15; Matt 10:1; Luke 9:1-2). The Twelve do indeed fulfill this mandate, but they are not the only ones who preach, heal, and exorcise demons. There is one incident, for example, where John complains to Jesus that an exorcist who was not among Jesus' followers was able to drive out demons (Mark 9:38-41; Luke 9:49-50). Jesus responds, "Do not stop him; for no one who does a deed of power in my name will be able soon afterward to speak evil of me. Whoever is not against us is for us" (Mark 9:39-40; similarly Luke 9:50).

When it comes to preaching, others besides the Twelve are commissioned by Jesus to proclaim the good news. Jesus tells a man who has been healed of demons, "Go home to your friends and tell them how much the

Lord has done for you, and what mercy he has shown you." This healed man "went away and began to proclaim [*kēryssein*] in the Decapolis how much Jesus had done for him" (Mark 5:19-20; Luke 8:39). Similarly, a man who was healed of leprosy (Mark 1:45) and one healed of deafness and a speech impediment (Mark 7:36) proclaimed *(kēryssein)* what Jesus had done.[4] In these instances, the same verb, *kēryssein* ("to proclaim, to preach") is used as for the proclaiming done by Jesus (Mark 1:14) and the Twelve (Mark 6:12). In all four gospels the Galilean women are also commissioned to proclaim. We will return to their stories momentarily.

Longtime Companion, Eyewitness, Commissioned to Proclaim

Another set of qualifications for an apostle is found in the Acts of the Apostles, when the community is choosing a replacement for Judas for the "ministry of apostleship" (1:25). They stipulate that it must be "one of the men who have accompanied us during all the time that the Lord Jesus went in and out among us, beginning from the baptism of John until the day when he was taken up from us" (1:21-22). Two criteria are articulated: Judas's replacement is to be a male *(anēr)* member of the community of believers and one who has been an eyewitness from the beginning. Paul and many other apostles named in his letters would not have fit this last criterion. Rather, Paul defines an apostle as one who has seen the risen Christ. Like the other New Testament writers, he also views an apostle as one who has been commissioned to proclaim the gospel. He argues in a rather circular manner that he has indeed been so commissioned from the evidence that the Corinthians have been brought to faith by his preaching (1 Cor 9:1-2). In his second letter to the Corinthians, when Paul's authority is being challenged by others whom he dubs "false apostles" (11:13) and "super-apostles" (12:11), he asserts that the "signs and wonders and mighty works" performed among them are the signs that he is a true apostle (2 Cor 12:12). Paul is especially clear about his commission in the opening of his letter to the Galatians: "Paul an apostle—sent neither by human commission nor from human authorities, but through Jesus Christ and God the Father,

---

4. In these two instances, Jesus did not send them to proclaim; rather, he insisted that they tell no one. In Matthew's version (8:1-4) the incident ends with Jesus' admonition not to tell anyone; Luke's account (5:12-16) concludes with a notice that "now more than ever the word about Jesus spread abroad," but it does not specify who is spreading the word.

who raised him from the dead" (Gal 1:1). Paul understands his particular commission to be apostle to the Gentiles (Rom 11:13; Gal 2:8).

The Galilean Women

In each of the gospels, Galilean women are commissioned to proclaim the good news. In Mark's Gospel, a heavenly messenger commissions Mary Magdalene, Mary the mother of James, and Salome, "Go, tell his disciples and Peter that he is going ahead of you to Galilee; there you will see him, just as he told you" (16:7). This Gospel, unlike the other three, ends, however, with the women saying nothing to anyone because they are afraid.[5] Mark leaves the story open-ended, inviting his hearers to take up the commission to go forth and proclaim the good news. In the Shorter Ending of Mark (NRSV), the women do tell Peter and the others all that had been commanded them, after which Jesus himself "sent out through them, from east to west, the sacred and imperishable proclamation of eternal salvation." In the Longer Ending, Jesus appears to Mary Magdalene, and she tells those who had been with him, but they do not believe (vv. 9–11). Then he appears to two nameless disciples as they were walking into the country, and they go back and tell the rest, but neither are they believed (vv. 12–13). Later he appears to the Eleven, upbraids them for not believing the previous ones who had seen him, and then commissions them, "Go into all the world and proclaim the good news to the whole creation" (v. 15).

In the Gospel of Matthew, it is Mary Magdalene and "the other Mary" who go to the tomb. They are commissioned to proclaim the good news to the other disciples both by the angel at the tomb (28:7) and by the risen Christ himself (28:10). That they do fulfill this command is implied by 28:8, where they run to tell the disciples, and 28:16, where the Eleven go to Galilee as they were directed. In the Gospel of Luke it is "Mary Magdalene, Joanna, Mary the mother of James, and the other women with them" who tell the apostles what they have heard from the angel at the tomb, but the other apostles did not believe them (Luke 24:9–11). In all four gospels, the constant figure at the crucifixion, burial, and empty tomb is Mary Magdalene. In the Gospel of John (20:1–18), she comes to the tomb alone. We will now look more closely at the Johannine account.

---

5. Most biblical scholars hold that Mark 16:8 is the original ending and that vv. 9–20 have been added later by other authors to round out the story.

Mary Magdalene: Apostle to the Apostles[6]

One of the favorite literary techniques of the Fourth Evangelist is to feature a single character who represents a whole group.[7] Nicodemus (3:1-21; 7:50-51; 19:38-42), for example, stands for all teachers who are sure they know, but who take a long time to commit to Jesus. The man born blind (9:1-41) represents those who are able to come to the light of faith. Thomas voices the doubts of all who have trouble believing unless they see (20:24-29). Mary Magdalene, coming alone to the tomb (20:1-18), represents the whole community of beloved disciples. It is the first day of the week, and it is still dark. The symbolism of light and darkness appears throughout this gospel to signify believing and inability to come to faith. Furthermore, belief is not instantaneous. In many scenes in this Gospel, including this one, a person comes to believe only after a lengthy discussion with Jesus, as he leads them to deeper and deeper understanding.

After seeing that the stone had been removed from the tomb, Mary runs to Simon Peter and the other disciple, the one whom Jesus loved, and tells them, "They have taken the Lord out of the tomb, and we do not know where they have laid him" (20:2). As a representative of the believing community, Mary speaks in the first person plural, using "we." She also sounds a very important theological theme. In this Gospel, the question of "where" Jesus is to be found is central. The first disciples ask Jesus, "Where are you staying?" (1:38). Jesus knows from where he has come and where he is going; those who oppose Jesus do not (8:14). Jesus' disciples can go where he goes (14:3, 4; 17:24), but not his opponents (7:34, 36; 8:21, 22). "Where" in this gospel is more than spatial or geographic; it connotes the communion between Jesus and the One who sent him, and between Jesus and his disciples. The question Mary voices at the tomb is that of the whole community of his followers: Where is Jesus to be found now?

The answer comes in two parts. In the first part, vv. 3-10, Peter and the other disciple[8] run to the tomb and see that the body is not there; they see

6. Much of this section is based on the analysis by Sandra M. Schneiders in *Written That You May Believe: Encountering Jesus in the Fourth Gospel*, rev. and exp. ed. (New York: Crossroad Publishing, 2003), 202-23.

7. See Raymond F. Collins, "The Representative Figures in the Fourth Gospel," *DRev* 94 (1976): 26-46, 118-32.

8. This disciple is not named and is elsewhere said to be the disciple Jesus loved. The Beloved Disciple, the authority behind the Gospel (21:24), appears in the Last Supper scene as the one reclining at Jesus' breast (13:23-26), at the crucifixion, where Jesus entrusts this

only the linen wrappings and the cloth that had been on Jesus' head rolled up in a place by itself. Like Moses,[9] who took off the veil from his face whenever he went up the mountain to meet God in glory (Exod 34:33-35), so Jesus, who has returned to God in glory, has put aside the veil of his flesh. When the other disciple with Peter sees this, he comes to belief (v. 8). It is not belief in the resurrection, as v. 9 asserts, for "as yet they did not understand the scripture, that he must rise from the dead." And then they simply returned to their homes (v. 10), which is not what a disciple does who has just come to belief in the resurrection! Rather, "believe" is used here to speak in a general sense about personal attachment to Jesus and readiness to do as he bids. Peter and the other disciple have received the first part of the answer to the question of where Jesus is now: he has returned to God to take up the glory he had before (see 17:5).

The second part of the answer comes in vv. 11-18. Mary Magdalene has remained outside the tomb, weeping. As she looks inside, she sees two angels in white, sitting where Jesus' body had been. Unlike in the Synoptic accounts, the angels are not the ones who tell Mary that Jesus has been raised. Nor do they commission her to proclaim this fact to the others. They simply ask her why she is weeping. Her response again focuses on "where" Jesus is. She says that they have taken away her Lord, and she is intent on knowing where they have laid him. Mary then turns and sees Jesus standing there but does not know it is he. Thinking him the gardener, she again voices her quest to know where Jesus has been laid. When he calls her name,[10] she recognizes him and responds, "Rabbouni," or "my Teacher," and receives his instruction not to cling to the way she knew him previously,[11] as he has ascended to the Father.[12] Where he is now to be found

---

disciple and his mother to one another (19:25-27), and in the boat with the disciples to whom the risen Christ appears at the sea of Tiberias (21:7). A rivalry between Peter and the Beloved Disciple climaxes in 21:20-23. That the name and gender of this disciple is never given allows any disciple to insert himself or herself into the place of the one who is closest to Jesus.

9. The theme of Jesus as the New Moses can be seen in John 1:17, 45; 3:14; 5:45-46; 6:32; 7:19, 22-23; 8:15; 9:28-29.

10. There is an echo of John 10:3-5, where the Good Shepherd knows his sheep and calls them by name.

11. For a comprehensive survey of interpretations of this verse, see Harold W. Attridge, "'Don't Be Touching Me': Recent Feminist Scholarship on Mary Magdalene," in *A Feminist Companion to John,* 2 vols., ed. Amy-Jill Levine, with Marianne Blickenstaff, FCNT 5 (Cleveland: Pilgrim Press, 2003), 2:140-66.

12. Schneiders (*Written That You May Believe,* 220) reads v. 17 as a question (there are no punctuation marks in the Greek text), "Am I as yet (or still) not ascended?" The implied

is in the brothers and sisters, the gathered community of his disciples. He commissions Mary to go to them and tell them, which she does. There is no hint in this gospel that she has not believed.

First to See the Risen Christ

It is clear that there are two strands of tradition in the New Testament regarding who was first to see the risen Christ and be commissioned by him to proclaim the good news. In the Gospels of Matthew and John, it is Mary Magdalene. In Luke and Paul, it is Peter. In Luke's account of the empty tomb, Mary and her companions are commissioned by the angelic messengers, not Jesus directly, and the proclamation of the women is regarded as "an idle tale" by the others (24:11). Peter then runs to the tomb, sees the linen cloths, and goes home amazed (24:12). In the next episode, when Cleopas and his companion run back to Jerusalem to tell the others they have encountered the risen Christ on the road to Emmaus, the other disciples greet them with the assertion, "The Lord has risen indeed, and he has appeared to Simon!" (24:34). There is, however, no account of an appearance of the risen Christ to Peter in Luke's gospel. It is an ancient piece of the tradition that Peter was the first. In Paul's first letter to the Corinthians, he lists all those to whom the risen Christ appeared. Heading the list is Cephas, the Aramaic name for Peter, followed by the Twelve, then "more than five hundred brothers and sisters at one time," then James, then all the apostles, and last of all, Paul himself (1 Cor 15:5–8). There is no mention of Mary Magdalene and her companions. This issue is important because the first to see the risen Christ is the one entrusted with authority and leadership of the believing community. That historically the first appearance and commissioning was to the women is most likely, since it is recounted in all four gospels, which are drawing from more than one source. Moreover, it would not have served the church well to invent as the basis of their proclamation the witness of women in a male-dominated culture. The rivalry between

---

answer is "No, you are indeed ascended, that is, glorified." Jesus is not suspended between resurrection and ascension and glorification. In the Fourth Gospel, unlike in Luke, which has forty days of appearances between the resurrection and ascension, and ten more days before Pentecost, the passion, death, resurrection, ascension, glorification, and giving of the Spirit is all one moment.

Mary Magdalene and Peter continues to play out in a number of non-canonical gospels.[13]

Ongoing Tradition

The tradition that Mary Magdalene was the first to proclaim the good news to the other apostles has been further developed in numerous legends and much artwork from the first century into the Middle Ages. Many legends tell of Mary going to southern France to preach and baptize. Some of these include Martha as her companion. Stained-glass windows from the late thirteenth century in the cathedral at Semur in Burgundy depict both Mary Magdalene and Martha preaching. In the early third century, Hippolytus of Rome wrote in his commentary on the Song of Songs (25.6, 7) that the women who meet the risen Christ "were made apostles to the apostles, having been sent by Christ." Many scholars think that Hippolytus is referring to Mary Magdalene, but it is likely he is thinking of Mary and Martha of Bethany.[14]

A Samaritan Apostle

Another woman in the Fourth Gospel also functions as an apostle: the Samaritan woman whom Jesus meets at a well (John 4:4-42).[15] In this Gospel, there is no call or sending of the Twelve. In fact, the Twelve do not appear at all as a group, except for two references to them at the end of the Bread of Life Discourse, where some have found Jesus' words too hard to take and he asks the Twelve, "Do you also wish to go away?" (6:67). Then Jesus remarks, "Did I not choose you, the twelve? Yet one of you is a devil" (6:70).

---

13. See, for example, the *Gospel of Mary,* preserved in a second-century Coptic manuscript, in which Peter declares he cannot believe the Savior would reveal himself to a woman and not to the men. Finally, Levi comes to Mary's defense and accuses Peter of having a hasty temper and being like their adversaries. At his urging, they finally go off and preach, as Mary had urged them to do. See further Karen L. King, "The Gospel of Mary Magdalene," in *Searching the Scriptures: A Feminist Commentary,* vol. 2, ed. E. Schüssler Fiorenza (New York: Crossroad Publishing, 1994), 601-34.

14. Mary Ann Beavis, "Reconsidering Mary of Bethany," *CBQ* 74 (2012): 283.

15. Much of this section is based on the interpretation by Sandra Schneiders in *Written That You May Believe,* 126-48.

Then Judas is identified as "one of the twelve" (6:71), as is Thomas at the end of the Gospel (20:24). The one who functions as a model apostle in this Gospel is the woman who brought many in her city to believe in Jesus through her testimony (4:39) and to seek to abide with him (4:40). She exemplifies the goal and purpose of this Gospel, "that you may come to believe that Jesus is the Messiah, the Son of God, and that through believing you may have life in his name" (20:31). The Samaritan woman achieves this for her city "because of [her] testimony," *dia ton logon* (literally, "through her word," 4:39). The theme of the word, *logos,* stands out from the very opening verses of this Gospel, where it is used to refer to Jesus himself. The desire of the Samaritans to have Jesus stay with *(menein)* them (v. 40) points ahead to the final discourse, where Jesus uses a metaphor of vine and branches to speak to his disciples about the necessity of abiding *(menein)* in him, as he is in them (15:1-11).

Coming to the Light

There are many skewed interpretations of the story of the Samaritan woman. Some think that it is a story of the healing of a sinner. Nowhere in the text, however, does it say the woman is a sinner.[16] Nor does Jesus say to her, as he does to the healed man at the pool of Bethsaida, "Do not sin any more" (5:14), or to the woman caught in adultery, "Go your way and from now on do not sin again" (8:11). Some commentators think that, because the woman comes to the well at noon, this indicates that she is an outcast and that she is trying to avoid encounter with others, who would not ordinarily come to the well at the hottest part of the day. This line of reasoning misses the theological symbolism of light and darkness that is so prominent in this Gospel. In the previous chapter, Nicodemus comes to Jesus at night and is unable to believe. By contrast, the woman comes at the lightest part of the day and gradually comes to full faith in Jesus. As with so many other episodes in this Gospel, there is a gradual process of mutual self-revelation, as the woman first sees Jesus simply as "a Jew" (v. 9), then wonders if he is "greater than our ancestor Jacob" (v. 12), then understands him to be "a prophet" (v. 19), and finally the Messiah (vv. 25-26), and with her townspeople, "the Savior of the world" (v. 42). Narratively, it does not make sense to think of the woman as a shunned sinner. If she were such a

---

16. Contrast Luke 7:37.

pariah, how is it that her townsfolk so readily listened to her and believed her word?

Married to False Gods

Nonetheless, many interpreters focus on the dialogue about the five husbands (vv. 16–19) as an indication that she is a sinner. Since this is part of a highly theological and symbolic exchange, these verses should also be read in that way. Like Mary Magdalene, the Samaritan woman is a representative character. She embodies all Samaria, whom Jesus is inviting into intimate relationship with the God of Israel. The five husbands can be taken as an allusion to the five false gods of the Assyrians that Samaria adopted when they were conquered by them (2 Kgs 17:13–34). In Hebrew, there is a word play on *ba'al,* which means both "husband" and "Lord," or "God." When Jesus affirms that the one she has now is not her "husband," he is saying that Samaria is not espoused to the God of Israel, as they should be. The metaphor of YHWH as the faithful husband and Israel as the bride who strays is used often by the prophets (see esp. Hos 2). The woman understands this allusion and responds, "I see that you are a prophet" (v. 19), and the discussion continues about the proper place for worship. Leading us to this interpretation are texts in the previous chapters that sound a marital theme: the wedding feast at Cana (2:1–12) and John the Baptist's declaration that he is the best man, not the bridegroom (3:27–30). In addition, the setting at a well, where a man and a woman meet, evokes stories of patriarchs or their servants who meet their future wives at a well, for example, Isaac and Rebekah (Gen 24:10–61), Jacob and Rachel (Gen 29:1–20), and Moses and Zipporah (Exod 2:16–22).

Bringing Others to Jesus

Some interpreters diminish the role of the Samaritan woman as apostle by asserting that she does not come to full belief in Jesus; she is still questioning when she says, "He cannot be the Messiah, can he?" (v. 29). And they point to the last two verses, which emphasize Jesus' own word over the woman's: "And many more believed because of his word. They said to the woman, 'It is no longer because of what you said that we believe, for we have heard for ourselves, and we know that this is truly the Savior of the world'" (vv. 41–42). Another way to read v. 29 is as a rhetorical question, "Is this not the Christ?" which invites the villagers, as well as the contemporary reader, to enter into their own journey of coming to faith in Jesus.[17]

As for the woman bringing her townsfolk to Jesus, this action conforms to a constant pattern in the Fourth Gospel: those who come to believe in Jesus bring others to him. In the opening chapter, John the Baptist directs two of his disciples to Jesus, and they follow him (1:35–39). One of them was Andrew, who then brings his brother Simon Peter to Jesus, using words similar to that of the Samaritan woman, "We have found the Messiah!" (1:41). At the end of the gospel, Mary Magdalene is sent to Jesus' brothers and sisters to bring them to belief in him as Risen One (20:17). So the Samaritan woman, who has come to belief, shares the good news with others and is a conduit of faith for them.

Photina, Enlightened One

Although the Samaritan woman is not so named in the Gospel, she has been called an apostle by several early church fathers. Origen (ca. 185–253/54), for example, referred to the Samaritan woman as an apostle and evangelist: "Christ sends the woman as an apostle to the inhabitants of the city because his words have inflamed this woman" (*Comm. S. Jean* 4.26–27). Theophylact of Bulgaria (ca. 1050–1108), archbishop of Ochrid and biblical commentator, also calls her an apostle, as well as "anointed with priesthood" (*Joan.* 4.28ff., PG 123:1241D). In Eastern tradition, the Samaritan woman has enjoyed very high regard, and she has been given the name Photina, "Enlightened One." Various legends about her have grown up. One tells of her living in Carthage, where she preached the gospel. Another says she was imprisoned, where she continued to preach, converted Nero's daughter, and was then flayed alive and thrown down a well. Another tradition is that her head was preserved in the Church of St. Paul Outside the Walls, which led Cardinal Cesare Baronius (1538–1607) to include her in the Roman martyrology. A chant from Byzantine tradition notes that she is "equal to the apostles":

---

17. Mary Coloe, *God Dwells with Us: Temple Symbolism in the Fourth Gospel* (Collegeville, MN: Liturgical Press, 2001), 106.

Thou wast illumined by the Holy Spirit
And refreshed by the streams of Christ the Saviour.
Having drunk the Water of Salvation
Thou didst give copiously to the thirsty.
O Holy Great Martyr Photina,
Equal-to-the-Apostles,
Entreat Christ our God that our souls may be saved.

Junia, Notable among the Apostles

[7]Greet Andronicus and Junia, my relatives who were in prison with me; they are prominent among the apostles, and they were in Christ before I was. (Rom 16:7)

The one woman who is explicitly named an apostle in the New Testament is Junia, who is among those whom Paul greets in Romans 16. She and Andronicus were relatives of Paul and were imprisoned with him, though he does not say where. It is not known what the precise relationship is between Andronicus and Junia. Were they husband and wife, like Prisca and Aquila? Brother and sister? Cousins? Although Paul says they were prominent among the apostles, nothing more is known about them.

There has been some confusion as to whether Andronicus's partner was a man or a woman. The name in the Greek text, *Iounian,* in the accusative case, can be either masculine or feminine. If the noun is taken as feminine, it would be the woman's name "Junia"; if it is considered masculine, it would be the man's name "Junias."[18] The evidence is overwhelmingly in favor of the name being that of a woman. Until now, the masculine name Junias has not been found in any Latin or Greek inscriptions or in any ancient literature, whereas the feminine name Junia is well-attested. Most telling is that early commentators on the letter to the Romans all took Junia to be a woman. John Chrysostom, for example, comments, "Indeed, how great the wisdom of this woman must have been that she was even deemed worthy of the title of apostle."[19] In addition, Origen of Alexandria,

18. Some modern translations, such as KJV, NAB, NRSV, have "Junia"; others, such as *La Biblia de las Américas,* NASB, and NJB, have "Junias." The RSV has "Andronicus and Junias . . . they are men of note among the apostles." The word "men," however, is not in the Greek text.
19. *In Epistolam ad Romanos,* Homilia 31.2 (PG 60:669-70).

Jerome (340/50-419/20), Hatto of Vercelli (924-961), Theophylact, and Peter Abelard (1079-1142) all understood Junia to be a woman.[20] Not until the thirteenth century did commentators begin to interpret the name as masculine, beginning with Aegidius of Rome (1245-1316). They presumed that a woman could not be an apostle, therefore the name had to be that of a man.

Women Apostles in Early Christian Tradition and Beyond

Many other women not named in Scripture were regarded as apostles in the early church. The *Acts of Thecla*, for example, written in Asia Minor in the late second century, tells of how Thecla, a rich aristocratic woman, renounced her family, fortune, and fiancé to accompany Paul in his missionary work. Devotion to Saint Thecla became widespread throughout Asia Minor and Egypt. Her image has been found painted on walls of tombs, stamped on clay flasks and oil lamps, and engraved on bronze crosses.[21] Another woman apostle, Nino, appears in several different works. The traditions about her are varied. One is that she received her theological education from a woman teacher in Jerusalem and was then given a cross and commissioned by Juvenal, the first patriarch of Jerusalem (451-58), to evangelize wherever she might go. Another tradition says that she traveled throughout Georgia, where she preached the gospel as a prisoner of war during the reign of Constantine. She is still highly revered in the Georgian Orthodox Church.

Although only one woman is explicitly named an apostle in the New Testament, other women are portrayed in the Gospels as having been commissioned by Jesus and acting in apostolic roles, such as the Samaritan woman and Mary Magdalene. Traditions about women such as Martha, Thecla, and Nino going out to preach and heal abound. Whereas only a few are remembered in written traditions, we can surmise that there were many others who spread the gospel as apostles whose names and stories are now lost to us. We can also envision that women were among the further seventy anonymous apostles that Jesus sent out in pairs in Luke 10:1-

20. For precise references, see Bernadette Brooten, "'Junia . . . Outstanding among the Apostles' (Romans 16:7)," in *Women Priests: A Catholic Commentary on the Vatican Declaration,* ed. Leonard Swidler and Arlene Swidler (New York: Paulist Press, 1977), 141-44.

21. See further Stephen J. Davis, *The Cult of St. Thecla: A Tradition of Women's Piety in Late Antiquity,* OECS (New York: Oxford University Press, 2001).

12. Seventy is a symbolic number that represents a full, complete number. In addition, in the Acts of the Apostles, it is not only the Eleven (named in 1:13) who are gathered in the upper room awaiting the Spirit who will empower them for mission, but also present are the "women, including Mary, the mother of Jesus" (1:14). The group of believers numbered 120 persons (1:15), symbolic of a full number, presumably both women and men, and they are all gathered in one place on the day of Pentecost (2:1). What the rest of Acts does not recount is how the women who are filled with the Spirit enact the apostolic mission. Instead, Peter and Paul take center stage. That women apostles did go forth in like manner is preserved in many extrabiblical traditions.

FOR DISCUSSION

1. What does the biblical record about women apostles say to you about ministry in the church today?
2. What misconceptions about the Samaritan woman and Mary Magdalene still linger? How might these be dispelled?
3. What cultural factors are at work in perceptions about women apostles, both ancient and contemporary?

FOR FURTHER READING

Brock, Ann Graham. *Mary Magdalene, the First Apostle: The Struggle for Authority.* Cambridge, MA: Harvard University Press, 2003.

Hearon, Holly E. *The Mary Magdalene Tradition: Witness and Counter-Witness in Early Christian Communities.* Collegeville, MN: Liturgical Press, 2004.

Levine, Amy-Jill, ed., with Marianne Blickenstaff. *A Feminist Companion to John.* 2 vols. FCNT 4–5. Cleveland: Pilgrim Press, 2003.

Schaberg, Jane. *The Resurrection of Mary Magdalene: Legends, Apocrypha, and the Christian Tradition.* New York: Continuum, 2002.

Schneiders, Sandra M. *Written That You May Believe: Encountering Jesus in the Fourth Gospel.* Rev. and exp. ed. New York: Crossroad, 2003.

CHAPTER 8

Pitting Mary against Martha:
Conflicts over Women's Roles

³⁸Now as they went on their way, he entered a certain village, where a woman named Martha welcomed him into her home. ³⁹She had a sister named Mary, who sat at the Lord's feet and listened to what he was saying. ⁴⁰But Martha was distracted by her many tasks; so she came to him and asked, "Lord, do you not care that my sister has left me to do all the work by myself? Tell her then to help me." ⁴¹But the Lord answered her, "Martha, Martha, you are worried and distracted by many things; ⁴²there is need of only one thing. Mary has chosen the better part, which will not be taken away from her."

LUKE 10:38-42

What's Wrong with This Picture?

When you hear this story of Martha and Mary, with whom do you most identify?[1] Many women who feel stretched by multiple demands on their time, as they balance work and family obligations, long for quiet time for themselves to be fed spiritually. They feel like Martha, and envy Mary. This gospel episode is very often interpreted in Bible commentaries and in preaching as a story that exemplifies the tension between contemplation and action. Jesus' pronouncement about Mary having chosen the better part is usually heard as an admonition to believers that, unless they take time to pray, they will not be able to live out the active demands of their

---

1. Much of the material in this chapter is based on chap. 11 of my book *Choosing the Better Part? Women in the Gospel of Luke* (Collegeville, MN: Liturgical Press, 1996), 144-62.

faith. While the tension between time for prayer and fulfillment of one's active duties is felt by most all of us, it is not entirely evident that this is the point of this particular gospel passage.

A host of questions arise when we probe beneath the surface. First, if the ideal in Christian life is to integrate contemplation and action, why are the two cast in opposition to one another, with Jesus approving one but not the other? Throughout the Gospel of Luke, there are repeated times when Jesus tells his disciples that both hearing and doing the word are necessary.[2] Another question is why Jesus, who is always compassionate to those who cry out to him in their difficulty, does not show any sympathy for Martha. The account seems to say that Jesus has no compassion for the way hard-working women struggle to balance all the demands on them. We might also ask why Martha did not address her complaint to Mary directly, and why Jesus let himself be drawn into a triangle where he had to side with one against the other.

The Nature of the Conflict

A key question is, What is the nature of the conflict between the two sisters? Some think the problem is that Martha is distracted by too many preoccupations, when all Jesus wants is for disciples to give him their attention. For some, the many things about which Martha is concerned are the many courses for the meal she is supposedly preparing, and Jesus only wants a simple supper. Some think that Mary and Martha are competing for Jesus' attention and that the conflict is fueled by sexual jealousy.[3] Another interpretation is that Jesus disapproves of Martha's anxiety and worry. Jesus warns his disciples that anxiety can stand in the way of their faith (Luke 8:14; 21:34) and repeatedly tells them not to worry (Luke 12:11, 22, 25). Jesus warns against anxiety about riches and pleasures of life (8:14), and he tells them not to worry about what to eat or what to wear (12:22; 21:34), or about what to say if brought before synagogues, rulers, and authorities (12:11). But none of these things are what trouble Martha; her preoccupation concerns much serving *(pollēn diakonian)*. She would appear to exemplify the attitude that Paul advocates for unmarried women or virgins: to be "anxious about the affairs of the Lord" (1 Cor 7:34).

2. E.g., Luke 6:47; 8:15, 21; 11:28.
3. Rachel Conrad Wahlberg, *Jesus according to a Woman* (New York: Paulist Press, 1976), 79.

Martha's Complaint

Crucial to understanding the nature of the conflict in Luke 10:38–42 and the source of Martha's anxiety is to know the meaning of the verb *diakonein* and the noun *diakonia* (see above, chap. 6). Both occur in v. 40: "But Martha was distracted by her many tasks [*diakonia*]; so she came to him and asked, 'Lord, do you not care that my sister has left me to do all the work [*diakonein*] by myself? Tell her then to help me.'" These terms are translated in various ways. The noun is rendered "tasks" (NRSV), "details of hospitality" (1970 ed. of the NAB), and "serving" (NAB, NJB, KJV). The verb is translated "do all the work" (NRSV), "do the serving" (NAB, NJB), and "serve" (KJV).

The verb *diakonein* and the noun *diakonia* together occur some nineteen times in Luke and Acts, denoting various kinds of ministerial service. This is the verb that epitomizes Jesus' mission and characterizes leadership in his movement, as Jesus says to his disciples at the Last Supper, "The greatest among you must become like the youngest, and the leader like one who serves [*ho diakonōn*]. For who is greater, the one who is at the table or the one who serves [*ho diakonōn*]? Is it not the one at the table? But I am among you as one who serves [*ho diakonōn*]" (22:26–27). As we saw above in chapter 6, the verb *diakonein* has a variety of ministerial connotations: it is used of the response of Simon's mother-in-law to Jesus after he heals her (Luke 4:39), and of the financial ministry of Mary Magdalene, Joanna, Susanna, and the other Galilean women (Luke 8:1–3). In Acts, *diakonia* refers to Paul's financial aid for the community in Jerusalem (11:29; 12:25) and to the whole of Paul's ministry (20:24; 21:19). It also denotes apostolic ministry (Acts 1:25), ministry of the table (Acts 6:2), and ministry of the word (Acts 6:4).

Seeing that *diakonein* and *diakonia* almost always refer to ministerial service in Luke and Acts,[4] it is likely that this is the meaning in Luke 10:40 as well. If this is the case, then Martha's concern is not that her sister is not helping her in the kitchen to prepare dinner,[5] but that Mary has been persuaded to give up more public diaconal ministry by those who advocated leaving these roles to the men. Although Mary and Martha were real figures in Jesus' life, it may be that this story is not giving us a historical vignette from the life of Jesus but, rather, reflects a conflict in the Lucan commu-

---

4. Two exceptions are when *diakonein* occurs in sayings about vigilant servants (Luke 12:37; 17:8). In these instances *diakonein* clearly refers to table service.

5. See Warren Carter, "Getting Martha out of the Kitchen: Luke 10:38-42," *CBQ* 58/2 (1996): 264-80. This essay also appears in Levine, *Feminist Companion to Luke*, 214-31.

nities. Luke uses Jesus' pronouncement as a vehicle to convey his answer to the question about women's roles in ministry. The conflict, then, is not between hearing and acting on the word. Both women welcome Jesus and his word. Martha welcomes Jesus into her home (v. 38),[6] and Mary listens receptively to Jesus' word (v. 39). What they do with what they hear is the source of conflict.

Conflicts over Women's Ministries

It is clear from the New Testament that there were women exercising ministerial leadership in the early Christian communities (see above, chap. 6). It is also clear that there were serious struggles over their ministry, which a number of texts in the Pauline and Deutero-Pauline letters reveal. One example is in Paul's first letter to the Corinthians:[7]

> [33]As in all the churches of the saints, [34]women should be silent in the churches. For they are not permitted to speak, but should be subordinate, as the law also says. [35]If there is anything they desire to know, let them ask their husbands at home. For it is shameful for a woman to speak in church. [36]Or did the word of God originate with you? Or are you the only ones it has reached? (1 Cor 14:33b-36)

This admonition seems to be at odds with the positive regard Paul expresses elsewhere for female coworkers and evangelizers. A number of scholars think that these verses were penned by someone other than Paul and were not originally part of the letter. One can see that vv. 33b-36 interrupt the flow of this section, which can easily be read without them. In addition, these verses contradict what Paul says earlier in the same letter, where he talks about women praying and prophesying in the assembly (1 Cor 11:2-16, see above, chap. 2). Whatever the problem was that he was addressing in that text, it is not that women are speaking in the gathering.

Another reason for questioning the authenticity of 14:33b-36 is that, in some Greek manuscripts, vv. 34-35 are found after v. 40, which suggests

---

6. This detail is a possible allusion to Martha being the head of a house church, like Mary, the mother of John Mark (Acts 12:12), Lydia (Acts 16:40), Prisca (Rom 16:5; 1 Cor 16:19), and Nympha (Col 4:15). Curiously, some of the ancient Greek manuscripts omit the phrase "into her home," possibly trying to diminish the leadership of Martha.

7. See further, Barbara E. Reid, "Problematic Paul on Women," *NTR* 5 (1992): 40-51.

they may have originated as a marginal note that then found its way into the text when different scribes inserted it into different places. Such scholars note the similarity in content and vocabulary to 1 Timothy 2:11-15, not thought to come from Paul himself. Finally, when Paul is attempting to persuade others to his point of view, he does not elsewhere appeal to the law in the way he does in v. 34. Taken together, these factors make a strong argument for vv. 33b-36 being a later addition.[8] However, attributing these verses to someone other than Paul only serves to make Paul more egalitarian. They are still in the canon and cannot simply be dismissed.

Other scholars believe vv. 33b-36 are original to Paul and to this letter but read them as part of a dialogue between Paul and the Corinthian men. They note that, in this section of 1 Corinthians, Paul is responding to questions the community has posed to him: "Now concerning the matters about which you wrote . . ." (1 Cor 7:1). In several places, Paul quotes what they have written before responding. For example, when he is trying to resolve the conflict over whether the Corinthians can eat meat sacrificed to idols, he quotes their words: "All things are lawful for me" (6:12; 10:23); "Food is meant for the stomach and the stomach for food" (6:13); and "No idol in the world really exists" and "there is no God but one" (8:4). Some translations, such as NRSV, put these slogans in quotation marks to make it clear what part of the dialogue is from the Corinthians. Verses 33b-36 can be seen as a similar kind of dialogue. It is the Corinthian men who are insisting that women keep silent in the churches and that they ask their husbands at home if they want to know something (vv. 34-35). Verse 36 is Paul's retort, upbraiding them, in effect: "What! Did the word of God originate with you [men]? Or are you the only ones it has reached?" In support of this interpretation, the Greek word *monous,* "only ones," is masculine. Additionally, the Greek particle *ē,* "or," at the beginning of v. 36, introduces a contradiction of the previous verses. Paul uses the same particle in this way in 1 Corinthians 11:20-22. Finally, in vv. 34-35 the use of the third person "they," "them," and "their" shows that it is the Corinthian men talking *about* the women. In v. 36 there is a switch to the second person plural "you," indicating that this verse is Paul's response to them. According to this interpretation, Paul is actually defending, not restricting, the right of the women to speak in the assembly.[9]

---

8. To indicate this conclusion, some translations, such as NRSV, place these verses in parentheses.

9. See N. Flanagan and E. Snyder, "Did Paul Put Down Women in 1 Cor 14:34-36?," *BTB*

Another line of interpretation is taken by scholars who understand 1 Corinthians 11:5 to refer to single women, while 1 Corinthians 14:33b-36 deals with married women. Because Paul has expressed his esteem for the unmarried, who he says can be single-minded about "the affairs of the Lord" and be "holy in body and spirit" (1 Cor 7:34), it is reasonable to think that the women prophets in 1 Corinthians 11:2-16 are unmarried. Paul approves of their speaking in the assembly. But in chapter 14 the situation may be that the wives were speaking out in ways that challenged the interpretations of the Scripture and prophecy being put forth by their own or other women's husbands, something that Paul considers to mitigate against good order. That he expects some pushback from the Corinthians, who know of married women like Prisca (see above, chap. 6), who would be leading and speaking out in the assembly, seems clear when he asserts that this is "a command of the Lord" and that "anyone who does not recognize this is not to be recognized" (14:37-38).[10]

Other scholars think that the two passages refer to two different contexts. The first (1 Cor 11:2-16) is a private house church gathering, where women may pray and prophesy freely in the assembly. The second (1 Cor 14:33b-36) is a citywide gathering of all the house churches who "come together" (1 Cor 11:16, 33; 14:26). In this more public, citywide gathering, women are to let the men do the speaking.[11] One other line of interpretation sees a distinction between the kinds of speaking. In 1 Corinthians 11:5 the women are praying and prophesying, which is an acceptable way of speaking in the assembly. In 1 Corinthians 14:34-35, some scholars think *lalein*, "speak," refers to gossiping or idle chat, which Paul prohibits.[12] One must question, however, whether this latter interpretation does not reveal sexist stereotypes. That the women are told to be subordinate and to ask their husbands at home, implies that they are asking important theological questions aloud, not chitchatting among themselves.

Whichever interpretation one adopts of 1 Corinthians 14:33b-36, one can say that there is ambiguity in Paul's letters in his attitudes toward

---

11 (1981): 10-12; D. Odell-Scott, "Let the Women Speak in Church: An Egalitarian Interpretation of 1 Cor 14:33b-36," *BTB* 13 (1983): 90-93.

10. Elisabeth Schüssler Fiorenza, *In Memory of Her: A Feminist Theological Reconstruction of Christian Origins* (New York: Crossroad Publishing, 1984), 230-33.

11. Vincent Branick, *The House Church in the Writings of Paul*, Zacchaeus Studies: New Testament (Wilmington: Glazier, 1989).

12. L. Scanzoni and N. Hardesty. *All We're Meant to Be: A Biblical Approach to Women's Liberation* (Waco, TX: Word Books, 1974).

women. At times he appears egalitarian (e.g., Gal 3:28; 1 Cor 11:11-12), while at others he insists on subordination of women to men (e.g., 1 Cor 11:3; 14:34; Col 3:18; Eph 5:22). His letters embody liberating attitudes toward women, as well as struggles to maintain traditional patriarchal practices. While he championed the equal status of women and men, slaves and free people, Jews and Greeks in terms of salvation in Christ, in his mind this perspective may not have translated into social equality. Paul, especially in his early letters, believes that the return of Christ is imminent (1 Cor 7:29-31) and thus advises that no one change his or her social situation with regard to circumcision, slavery, or marital status (1 Cor 7:17-40).

Attempts to Restrict and Control Women

If there is ambiguity about women's roles in the letters Paul himself wrote, such is not the case with the letters that later authors wrote in his name and with the mantle of his authority.[13] These clearly advocate submission of women to men and restrictions on women's ministry. In addition to the household codes (Col 3:18-4:1, Eph 5:21-6:9, 1 Pet 3:1-7), which we examined above in chapter 2, the Pastoral Letters show a strong effort to reinforce patriarchal structures in the church at the turn of the first century. Although the pastor lauds Timothy's mother and grandmother, Eunice and Lois (2 Tim 1:5) for having transmitted "sincere faith" to him, he does not advocate women teaching, preaching, or holding positions of authority. Rather, he asserts, "Let a woman learn in silence with full submission. I permit no woman to teach or to have authority over a man; she is to keep silent" (1 Tim 2:11-12). The justification he uses is that Eve was formed after Adam and was the one who was deceived and became a transgressor (see above, chap. 2). For him, the way to salvation for women is through childbearing (1 Tim 2:15). Similarly for the author of the letter to Titus, the ideal older woman is one who teaches younger women to love their husbands and children and be good homemakers (Titus 2:3-5).

That many women had nonetheless devoted themselves to ministry in the church is evident from the lengthy admonitions in 1 Timothy 5:3-16 that impose restrictions on their activities. There were celibate women, many of whom lived together, dedicating themselves to prayer, charitable work,

---

13. Most scholars hold that 2 Thessalonians, Ephesians, 1-2 Timothy, Titus, and possibly Colossians were not written by Paul himself.

and teaching who were compensated for their ministry by the church. Such women, who lived outside of the control of a husband, father, or other male relative, included widows, women who were separated or divorced from their husbands, and women who had never married.[14] The pastor attempts to contain their growing numbers and influence by imposing qualifications for those who aspire to belong to the ministering widows. First, he insists that a woman who has children and grandchildren be supported by her family and not the church (1 Tim 5:3-8).[15] To be enrolled as a widow, a woman must be sixty years old and married only once (1 Tim 5:9). Since most people in the first century did not live past forty, this qualification would be very difficult to meet. Moreover, many women were married in their teens to older men and then remarried when their husband died. The scenario in Mark 12:18-23, where a widow married seven different times is not so far-fetched. The pastor wants to see younger widows remarry and have more children and devote themselves to their households (1 Tim 5:14) rather than take up a life of ministry. But for those who do become enrolled as widows, he would have their ministry restricted to prayer (v. 5) and good works (v. 10). Finally, he concludes, any woman believer who "has widows" (v. 16),[16] that is, who oversees a house of widows (like Tabitha in Acts 9:36-43), is to assume their financial support rather than look to the church for compensation for their ministries.

Luke and Women

We can see that many New Testament texts give witness to the struggles in the early church around the ministries of women. Luke weighs in with those who think that the "better part" for women is to listen silently at

14. Joanna Dewey, "1 Timothy," in *Women's Bible Commentary*, ed. Carol A. Newsom, Sharon H. Ringe, and Jacqueline E. Lapsley, 3d rev. ed. (Louisville: Westminster John Knox, 2012), 599.

15. While most translations of 1 Tim 5:3 have "honor widows," the verb *timaō* also means "to set a price on" (BDAG, 1005), which here would mean "pay widows."

16. The expression *echei chēras* literally means "has widows." This meaning is obscured by translations such as "has relatives who are widows" (NRSV) or "has widowed relatives" (NAB, NJB). The NASB captures the sense well: "has dependent widows." While the KJV renders *echei chēras* well, "if any man or woman that believeth have widows," it incorrectly translates *tis pistē* as "any man or woman." The adjective *pistē* is feminine singular, "any believing woman."

the feet of Jesus, like Mary, not ministering in public ways, as Martha was doing. In his Gospel and Acts,[17] Luke features male disciples as the ones who are called and commissioned.[18] Like Jesus, they preach, teach, heal, exorcise, forgive, pray, endure persecution, and minister by the power of the Spirit.[19] Women are not depicted as doing any of these ministries in Luke and Acts. The powerfully prophetic women Elizabeth, Mary, and Anna in the infancy narratives are cast in the mold of the women prophets of the Old Testament, but not as disciples of Jesus.[20] In the rest of the Gospel, women such as Martha (10:40), the woman in the crowd (11:27-28), and Mary Magdalene, Joanna, and Mary (24:11), who speak out, are reprimanded by Jesus or are not believed.

Upholding Women's Theological Scholarship

Nonetheless, some scholars read Jesus' affirmation of Mary in Luke 10:38-42 as a stride forward for women, seeing this as approval for women to abandon traditional domestic roles and learn theology. Just as Paul studied the law at the feet of Gamaliel (Acts 22:3), so Mary's sitting at the feet of Jesus to be tutored by him opens the way for women theologians. Some even go so far as to say this is an unheard of, even revolutionary, move. However, in the Hellenistic period, formal education of women was beginning to be more acceptable, especially for women from elite Roman families. An ideal

17. A number of scholars question whether the Third Gospel and Acts of the Apostles were written by the same person. For our purposes, since the author of Acts clearly intends it to be the companion volume to the gospel, addressed to the same patron, Theophilus, we will speak of Luke as author as both.

18. Because the Third Gospel has more stories that feature women than any of the other gospels, some scholars, like Alfred Plummer (*The Gospel according to S. Luke,* 5th ed., ICC [Edinburgh: T&T Clark, 1981], xlii-xliii), have declared it to be "the Gospel for women." Others, such as Robert O'Toole (*The Unity of Luke's Theology: An Analysis of Luke-Acts,* GNS 9 [Wilmington: Glazier, 1984], 120), noting the way Luke constructs parallel pairs of stories of men and women, think that Luke regards women and men as equals. A number of feminist scholars, however, have concluded that Luke's portrayal of women is ambiguous at best (e.g., Turid Karlsen Seim, *The Double Message: Patterns of Gender in Luke-Acts* [Nashville: Abingdon Press, 1994]), and dangerous at worst (e.g., Elisabeth Schüssler Fiorenza, *In Memory of Her,* 50; Jane D. Schaberg and Sharon H. Ringe, "Luke," in *Women's Bible Commentary,* 492).

19. For more details, see chapter 3 in my book *Choosing the Better Part.*

20. Not until Acts 1:14, where the disciples are awaiting the Spirit, is Mary, the mother of Jesus, part of the group of Jesus' disciples.

woman in the eyes of Martial, a first-century Roman epigrammatist, is not only rich, noble, and chaste, but also erudite. In the writings of Juvenal, a Roman poet and satirist from the late first and early second century, we find evidence that, in some circles, educated women ate with men and were able to converse intelligently.[21] Another first-century Roman, Musonius Rufus, advocated education for women in his essay "That Women Too Should Study Philosophy." Further evidence of women's education is found in the various epigrams, poems, historical memoirs, rhetorical letters, and philosophical treatises written by Hellenistic women.[22]

Some commentators assert that Jewish tradition barred theological education for women and that Jesus broke open these restrictions by teaching Mary. Two of Rabbi Eliezer's sayings are often cited: "If any man gives his daughter a knowledge of the Law, it is as though he taught her lechery" (m. Sotah 3:4), and "Better to burn the Torah than place it in the mouth of a woman" (t. Sotah 21b).[23] This approach is highly problematic for a number of reasons. First, it results in the liberation of Christian women through vilification of Judaism, overlooking the fact that Jesus was a Jew and that his mission was a renewal movement *within* Judaism.[24] Second, these texts from the Mishnah date to around the year 200 CE, some 175 years after Jesus' ministry. We cannot say with certainty that Rabbi Eliezer's opinion reflected the thinking of Jews in Jesus' day. Moreover, the very same kinds of statements are made by early church fathers, whose work is closer to the time of the rabbis. Finally, to quote only Rabbi Eliezer is to give only part of the evidence. The same tractate of the Mishnah also contains the opinion of Ben Azzai, who says, "A man ought to give his daughter a knowledge of the Law" (m. Sotah 3:4). Similarly, m. Nedarim 4:3 declares it a religious duty to educate daughters as well as sons. More contemporary with the time of Jesus is the first-century Jewish philosopher Philo of Alexandria,

---

21. See Sarah B. Pomeroy, *Goddesses, Whores, Wives, and Slaves: Women in Classical Antiquity* (New York: Dorset, 1975), 172.

22. See Mary Lefkowitz, "Did Ancient Women Write Novels?," in *"Women like This": New Perspectives on Jewish Women in the Greco-Roman World,* ed. Amy-Jill Levine (Atlanta: Scholars Press, 1991), 208-11.

23. Rabbi Eliezer ben Hyrcanus was a prominent teacher in the late first and early second centuries and is one of the most frequently-mentioned rabbis in the Mishnah.

24. For an excellent resource to better understand Jesus within Judaism, see Amy-Jill Levine, *The Misundertood Jew: The Church and the Scandal of the Jewish Jesus* (San Francisco: Harper One, 2006). See also *The Jewish Annotated New Testament,* ed. Amy-Jill Levine and Marc Zvi Brettler (Oxford: Oxford University Press, 2011).

who describes the *Therapeutrides,* women ascetics who dedicated their lives to the study of Torah (Philo, *Vit. Cont.* 68). There is also evidence from the first century BCE through the sixth century CE that Jewish women were leaders of synagogues, a position that would have required them to be educated in Torah.[25]

One final consideration about this interpretation is that it upholds Mary's theological education at the expense of Mary's ministerial service. Nowhere else in Luke's Gospel does Jesus advocate contemplation over action or theological study over ministerial service. It is always both/and. The ideal disciple in Luke both hears and acts on the word.

Resistant Readings

To read the Lucan story about Mary and Martha as reflecting conflicts about women's ministries in the early church opens up new possibilities for giving a different answer than the one Luke did. It is interesting that, when we examine the ancient Greek manuscripts of Luke, we can see that many early copyists had difficulty with Jesus' definitive pronouncement that Mary had chosen the better part. While the oldest manuscript of Luke's Gospel has Jesus saying, "There is need of only one thing" (v. 42), others soften the saying by replacing "one thing" with "a few things." In some manuscripts the two readings are combined, making it nonsensical: "but of a few things there is need, or of one." Finally, some copyists omitted the whole phrase altogether, probably because of its incomprehensibility.[26] These variations show that there was not ready acceptance of the preference of Mary over Martha.

John 11:1–12:11

In the one other place in the Gospels where Martha and Mary appear, John 11:1–12:11, a very different portrait emerges. In the first scene, the raising of Lazarus (11:1–44), Martha plays a leading role. In the second, the anointing

25. See Bernadette Brooten, *Women Leaders in the Ancient Synagogue: Inscriptional Evidence and Background Issues,* BJS 36 (Chico, CA: Scholars Press, 1982), who analyzes nineteen inscriptions from Asia Minor, Crete, Italy, Greece, Thrace, Egypt, and Palestine.

26. See Bruce Metzger, *A Textual Commentary on the Greek New Testament,* 3d ed. (London: United Bible Societies, 1971), 153-54.

of Jesus (12:1–11), Mary comes to the fore. Both scenes are at a critical turning point in the gospel. Unlike the Synoptic Gospels, where the episode in the temple (Matt 21:12–17; Mark 11:15–19; Luke 19:45–48) is the last straw that galvanizes Jesus' opponents to move to put him to death, in the Fourth Gospel, it is the raising of Lazarus (11:45–54). Mary's anointing of Jesus' feet anticipates his burial and mirrors his ministrations to his disciples' feet at the Last Supper. In this Gospel, there is no tension or rivalry between the two sisters.

At the beginning of the episode, the evangelist underscores how much Jesus loved "Martha and her sister and Lazarus" (11:5).[27] It is notable that Martha is placed first in the trio. That Mary is not named and is identified in relation to Martha adds to Martha's prominence. In a gospel where the anonymous Beloved Disciple is the model disciple, it is significant that Martha is also introduced as "beloved."

As the story progresses, Martha is the one who goes out to meet Jesus when she heard that he was coming, while Mary stays at home (v. 20). In the dialogue that ensues, Martha, like many other characters in this gospel, moves to a deep theological understanding through the exchange with Jesus, which comes to a climax with her declaration, "Yes, Lord, I believe that you are the Messiah, the Son of God, the one coming into the world" (11:27). In the Synoptic Gospels, this confession of faith is made by Peter (Matt 16:16; Mark 8:29; Luke 9:20). In the Fourth Gospel his role is overshadowed by that of the Beloved Disciple, as well as by Martha, the Samaritan woman, and Mary Magdalene. Martha's profession of faith makes her a model believer, achieving the stated purpose of the evangelist, "that you may come to believe that Jesus is the Messiah, the Son of God, and that through this belief you may have life in his name" (20:31). It is also important to note that Martha makes this pronouncement before Jesus raises Lazarus from the dead. She exemplifies one who believes on the basis of Jesus' word, without seeing signs (see John 20:29). Martha's faith is then expressed in ministry. She serves *(diēkonei)* at the dinner party given at their home after Lazarus has been raised (12:1–11).

It is evident from the way that the Fourth Evangelist depicts Martha and Mary, as beloved and model disciples, as well as the Samaritan woman and Mary Magdalene as apostles, preachers, and evangelizers (see above, chap. 7), that this community has adopted different attitudes and practices toward women from the communities behind the Synoptic Gospels. There

---

27. Jesus' love for Lazarus is noted two other times, in vv. 3 and 36.

are still tensions over the leadership of women (as voiced in John 4:27 by the male disciples, who object to Jesus talking to the Samaritan woman, and by Judas in John 12:5, who complains about Mary wasting the perfume). But unlike Luke, who has Jesus side with those who would restrict women's roles, the Johannine Jesus defends women's ministerial actions (12:7-8).

Other Traditions about Martha and Mary

Many other traditions from the early church and into medieval times uphold Martha's ministerial leadership. In a number of texts and in various depictions of the myrrh-bearing women, Martha is among the women who go to Jesus' tomb to anoint his body. In the Coptic version of *Epistula Apostolorum,* dating to the early second century, it is Martha who is sent as the first apostle of the resurrection. Likewise, Hippolytus of Rome (early third century), in his *Commentary on the Song of Songs,* calls Martha and Mary "apostles to the apostles" (25.6, 7).[28] In these and other texts, it is Martha who is named first and who takes the lead role.[29] In two other works dating to the fourth century, *Apostolic Church Order* and *Acts of Philip,* Martha is exercising her *diakonia* in a eucharistic context. One other notable instance is a sermon that may be by Bernard of Clairvaux (1090-1153), in which "Martha was held up as a model for prelates."[30] In the Middle Ages, Dominican mystic Meister Eckhart (ca. 1260-1327) saw Martha as the one who had already reached the stage of integrating contemplation and action, while Mary was still a novice in the contemplative life. He wrote:

> Martha, being firmly established in virtue, open-minded, not hindered by things, wanted her sister to be like her, for she realised her insecurity. She had the highest motives, wishing her all that pertains to eternal felicity. . . . Martha feared that her sister would stay dallying with pleasure and sweetness, so Christ says in effect: All is well, Martha, she has cho-

28. As pointed out by Mary Ann Beavis, "Mary of Bethany and the Hermeneutics of Remembrance," *CBQ* 75 (2013): 746.

29. See further Allie M. Ernst, *Martha from the Margins: The Authority of Martha in Early Christian Tradition,* SVC 98 (Leiden: Brill, 2009).

30. Giles Constable, *Three Studies in Medieval Religious and Social Thought* (Cambridge: Cambridge University Press, 1995), 92. I am indebted to Robert J. Karris for this reference in his review of my book *Choosing the Better Part,* in *JBL* 117/3 (1998): 539-41.

sen the best part, this will pass. The best that can befall creatures lies in store for her; she shall be blessed like thee.[31]

Similarly, in medieval interpretations, "Monastic authors were particularly attracted to the view of Martha and Mary as two contrasting but complementary, and not necessarily mutually exclusive, types of life or people."[32] A number of medieval paintings dating from the fourteenth to the sixteenth centuries highlight Martha's active service, putting her in a pose akin to that of St. George—killing a dragon![33] In one of the works of Fra Angelico (1387–1455), Martha and Mary are painted into the scene at Gethsemane. On the left, Jesus is kneeling upright, while Peter, James, and John are asleep. Mary, meanwhile is looking down at a book, but Martha mirrors Jesus' pose. She is upright, with her hands together like his, uplifted in prayer. Another painting of Fra Angelico depicts Martha with Veronica at the foot of the cross, again affirming Martha's active following of Jesus.

Both Are Good

While Luke 10:38–42 may have functioned to advocate silent, passive, contemplative roles for women, it is clear that there have always been women and men in the church who resisted such restrictions on women's ministries. Today as feminists critique binary oppositions and dualistic either/or thinking, we might think instead of the importance of both sisters and their choices. We might note that in v. 42, Jesus does not use the comparative "better" but says, literally, "Mary has chosen the good [*agathēn*] part."[34] Moreover, Jesus does not tell Martha that her choice is not important or valuable. He simply remarks on her anxiety and points her to the one thing

31. Meister Eckhart, "A Sermon on the Contemplative and the Active Life," in *Late Medieval Mysticism*, ed. Ray C. Petry (Philadelphia: Westminster, 1957), 197. My thanks for this reference to Loveday C. Alexander, "Sisters in Adversity: Retelling Martha's Story," in *A Feminist Companion to Luke*, ed. Amy-Jill Levine, with Marianne Blickenstaff, FCNT 3 (Sheffield: Sheffield Academic Press, 2002), 204.

32. Constable, *Three Studies*, 16.

33. See Elisabeth Moltmann-Wendel, *The Women around Jesus* (New York: Crossroad Publishing, 1987), 14–48.

34. So the RSV translation. As Joseph A. Fitzmyer (*The Gospel according to Luke X–XXIV*, AB 28A [Garden City: Doubleday, 1985], 894) notes, "The positive degree of the adj. is often used in Hellenistic Greek for either the superlative or comparative, both of which were on the wane." However, the comparative sense is not demanded.

necessary. Another way of reading Luke 10:38–42 is that both Martha's choice and Mary's are good and must be upheld.

FOR DISCUSSION

1. How would you rewrite the ending of the story in Luke 10:38–42?
2. How do you experience and respond to the tensions over women's leadership in ministry?
3. How are both contemplative listening and active service equally essential for a disciple?

FOR FURTHER READING

Ernst, Allie M. *Martha from the Margins: The Authority of Martha in Early Christian Tradition.* SVC 98. Leiden: Brill, 2009.

Levine, Amy-Jill, ed., with Marianne Blickenstaff. *A Feminist Companion to Luke.* FCNT 3. Sheffield: Sheffield Academic Press, 2002.

———. *A Feminist Companion to the Deutero-Pauline Epistles.* FCNT 7. London: T&T Clark, 2003.

Reid, Barbara. *Choosing the Better Part? Women in the Gospel of Luke.* Collegeville, MN: Liturgical Press, 1996.

Seim, Turid Karlsen, *The Double Message: Patterns of Gender in Luke-Acts.* Nashville: Abingdon, 1994.

CHAPTER 9

From Death to New Life

Taking Up the Cross

One of the most challenging things that a Christian faces is how to make sense of the death of Jesus and to live into what that means. In recent years, feminist biblical scholars and theologians have examined the ways in which some interpretations of the cross can be deadly for women. In this chapter we will look first at the way the Gospel of Mark portrays Jesus' passion and death, and then we will turn to the Fourth Gospel. We will look at the ways in which there are both pitfalls and promise in each interpretation.

Ask most any Christian why Jesus died, and the response comes readily, "He died for our sins." Although this formulation is found in Paul's first letter to the Corinthians (15:3), it is only one of many ways in which Paul interprets the cross. This interpretation gained prominence in the late eleventh and early twelfth centuries when Anselm, bishop of Canterbury (1033-1109), developed the theology of atonement. It has proved to be the one that has stuck with most people, even though it is not the way most New Testament authors present Jesus' death. In addition, many Christians have lost sight of the way that Anselm tried to keep God's love at the center, and they think instead of an angry God who must be appeased for our sins, or of human sin being so great that only the Son of God could atone for it. Neither one of these interpretations is true to the Scriptures.

Jesus' Passion and Death according to the Gospel of Mark

A Dangerous Saying

He called the crowd with his disciples, and said to them, "If any want to become my followers, let them deny themselves and take up their cross and follow me." (Mark 8:34)

These familiar words of Jesus come on the heels of Peter's declaration of Jesus as Messiah and Jesus' first predication of the passion (Mark 8:27-33).[1] Peter rejects what Jesus says about suffering and dying, and then Jesus rebukes him. He voices the struggle of all disciples to understand and accept the cross. But there are some so-called crosses that should not be accepted. One of my students in a course on the Gospel of Mark once brought this point home forcefully. We were talking about what taking up the cross might mean today for those of us who don't face any physical danger for being a disciple of Jesus. At the back of the room, one of my students raised her hand insistently. When I called on her, she declared that Mark 8:34 is the deadliest verse in the whole Bible and she wished we could rip it out and never proclaim it again! I was startled and struggled to understand what she meant. When I asked her if she could say more, she explained that she worked in a shelter for battered women. In her experience, the biggest obstacle for Christian women to come for help when they were being abused was this verse of the Gospel. Many women, she told me, when they finally reach the point of deciding to break the silence about what is happening in their homes, confide in their priest or minister. More often than not, he will quote Paul's admonition, "Wives, be subject to your husbands" (Col 3:18) and advise her to go home and to take whatever abuse her husband heaps on her as her way of carrying the cross with Jesus. The class was stunned at such an interpretation. How could the cross, the symbol of salvation and liberation, be construed in such a deadly way?

A second example highlights the ways in which many women have interiorized an understanding of the cross that has kept them locked in oppressive situations, squelching any movement toward trying to confront or change things for the better. Several years ago I had the opportunity to meet women in the diocese of San Cristóbal de las Casas, in the

---

1. This section is based on my book *Taking Up the Cross: New Testament Interpretations through Latina and Feminist Eyes* (Minneapolis: Fortress Press, 2007).

state of Chiapas, Mexico. This diocese has a vibrant network of women's Bible study groups coordinated by Coordinación Diocesana de Mujeres (CODIMUJ), the diocesan office for women. Through study of the Scriptures "with the mind, eyes, and heart of a woman," many women are learning to analyze their reality and act in liberating ways. One woman described how she and many other women had understood Jesus' sacrifice on the cross as translated into their own lives:

> He taught us how to sacrifice, how to give our lives for others, how to be humble and not self-centered. We sacrifice especially for our children, for our husbands, for our families. When there is not enough food, we give the best portions to our children and husbands. We sacrifice so our children can go to school, selling whatever we can in the market. We do not follow our own desires, but offer up our lives for theirs.[2]

Another woman describes her daily sacrifices:

> I cannot read or write; I have to be content with knowing how to cook and sew. I get up at four o'clock every morning to get water and gather wood and start the fire for breakfast. I do all the housework and I work in the fields alongside my husband as well, with my youngest baby strapped to my back. I get no pay for any of my work. Men can spend money as they wish, and many waste it on drink; we women are completely dependent on what our husbands give us. At the end of the day, my husband relaxes while I keep tending the children and fix dinner. Afterward there is more work to prepare for the next day. I don't ever rest or have a day off. Who would carry out my responsibilities? God has made it this way, we have to be humble and sacrifice for others.

Reading with the Mind, Eyes, and Heart of a Woman

Observing the deadly effects of such attitudes based on misreadings of the Scriptures and deeply ingrained cultures of subjugation of women, groups of women, with the encouragement of Don Samuel Ruiz, bishop of San Cristóbal de las Casas from 1959-1999, began to study the Bible from their

---

2. This and the next two quotations are from women in CODIMUJ, whose reflections are recorded in *Con mirada, mente y corazón de mujer* (Mexico City: CODIMUJ, 1999), 17-22.

own perspective. When they read the text with the mind, eyes, and heart of a woman, different interpretations began to emerge. One woman described it this way:

> The worst thing was that we women regarded this situation as natural. We believed that this is just the way things are; there is nothing that can be done about it. We felt trapped; we never thought of ourselves as having value in ourselves, or of being capable and free to make choices and decisions about our own lives. Sorrowful, solitary, silent, and enclosed: this was our reality inside our homes in our daily lives—lives that we did not choose and that we thought we had no way to change. In our prayer we would cry to God asking why he had determined this life for us. Our faith did not help us change anything; we believed that God had decided that it should be so. All the suffering we endured we accepted as our way of carrying the cross.

Not only in rural Chiapas does one find such theological interpretations of the cross. In many Christian communities around the globe, women can be heard to make similar statements. As we turn to Mark's Gospel and look with feminist eyes, we ask, Where is the freeing message of the gospel for those who suffer unjustly?

The Marcan Context

When we look at Mark 8:34 in the literary and theological context of the Gospel, it becomes clear that, when Jesus invites disciples to take up their cross, he is speaking of a very particular kind of suffering. "Taking up the cross" does not refer to passive acceptance of all kinds of suffering. It refers specifically to the willingness of disciples to expose themselves to the possible negative repercussions for living and proclaiming the gospel, even to accept death, if necessary. This means that suffering that comes from injustice or abuse is not "a cross" that should be borne; rather, every effort should be made to counter and stop it. Likewise, suffering that can befall any human being, such as sickness and death, is not technically a "cross," though Christians derive strength and comfort from identifying such suffering with that of Jesus.

When Jesus utters this saying in Mark's Gospel, it comes at a crucial turning point in the narrative. In the first eight chapters, Jesus has been preaching, teaching, healing, exorcising demons, feeding multitudes, and creating a new family of disciples throughout Galilee. There is an aura of mystery throughout, as Jesus' disciples repeatedly misunderstand him,[3] and he continually admonishes people not to say anything to anyone about him yet.[4] This literary theme of secrecy heightens the suspense in the narrative, and it also serves an important theological purpose: until one gets to the end of the story and comes to grips with the cross and empty tomb, one is not able to adequately proclaim the Christ. To speak only of his deeds of power is just part of the picture. The themes of secrecy and misunderstanding reach a climax when Jesus puts the question to his disciples: "Who do people say that I am?" (8:27). They tell him, "John the Baptist; and others, Elijah; and still others, one of the prophets" (v. 28). Then he asks them, "But who do you say that I am?" Peter pipes up with the correct answer: "You are the Messiah" (v. 29), and immediately Jesus orders the disciples "not to tell anyone about him" (v. 30). He then begins to teach them about his impending passion (vv. 31-33), which Peter vigorously rejects (v. 32). Twice more Jesus will speak to them about his passion (9:30-32; 10:32-34), each time followed by an episode in which the disciples misunderstand, arguing over who is the greatest (9:33-37) and asking for places of honor (10:35-45). The cross has been looming since the beginning of the Gospel. As early as 3:6 the Pharisees and Herodians are conspiring against Jesus to destroy him. But the first explicit speech of Jesus about his suffering and death comes only in chapter 8, as an explanation of the type of Messiah he is. In this context Jesus speaks to his disciples about denying themselves and taking up the cross to follow him.

Denial of Self vs. Self-Denial

Another important aspect of the saying in Mark 8:34 is the meaning of denial of self. Jesus is speaking to the disciples not about practices of self-denial, such as forgoing something enjoyable, like eating candy, during Lent. Rather, he is talking about embracing a way of life in which one places at the center God's realm and the well-being of the whole body of Christ and the whole of the cosmos. Such a life requires self-surrender in love and service to the most vulnerable. Denial of self does not mean

3. See, e.g., Mark 4:13, 41; 6:51-52; 7:17-18; 8:21, 32; 9:10, 34; 10:35-38.
4. Mark 1:44; 3:12; 5:43; 7:36; 8:26.

the obliteration of one's self in subservience and submission, such as the women in Chiapas had done. Nor does it entail the loss of one's identity or ignoring legitimate needs. Denial of self, in the gospel sense, means cultivating a healthy sense of self-worth and giftedness, and freely choosing to surrender one's self in the service of love.

An example of such surrender of self out of love can be seen in the following example, which occurred in one of the villages in Chiapas. It happened that a woman who had gone to one of the women's Bible study meetings returned to her home to find her husband drunk and infuriated that she was not there to serve him his coffee when he wanted it. He beat her badly, as he had many times before. When her friends saw her bruised face and battered body the next day, they decided that they would act in self-surrender, motivated by love for their friend. Thirty strong, these women came to the house and confronted the abusive husband. They threatened that, if he ever laid a hand on his wife again, *he* would end up the one bruised and battered. While one would prefer not to return violence for violence, the powerful presence and words of the women had the desired effect. The husband was shocked into getting the help he needed to give up drinking and to stop his abusive behavior. For the women in this village, their understanding of "denying themselves" and "taking up the cross" had rightly shifted away from a self-abnegation whereby they simply accepted all forms of suffering, even abuse, to an empowered self-surrender leading to service to another, motivated by love, aimed at ending abuse.

Silent Suffering Servant

One of the images that comes through strongly in the Marcan passion narrative is the likeness of Jesus to the silent, suffering servant in Isaiah. Throughout the interrogation and trial by Pilate, Jesus does not respond, just as the Isaian servant did not: "He was oppressed, and he was afflicted, yet he did not open his mouth; like a lamb that is led to the slaughter, and like a sheep that before its shearers is silent, so he did not open his mouth" (Isa 53:7). Not only is Jesus voiceless before his accusers, but God too seems to be silent. In Mark's version of the prayer in Gethsemane, Jesus receives no response from God to his anguished prayer to let the cup pass (14:32-42), and there is no answer to his final words on the cross, "My God, my God, why have you forsaken me?" (15:34). While these words might sound like

Jesus dies in despair, they are actually the first line of Psalm 22, a lament psalm uttered by one who is suffering as the victim of injustice, and who trusts ultimately in God to bring vindication. When Jesus seems to have no answer as to how God will bring about joy and goodness and freedom for humankind through his horrific death, he abandons himself in total trust to God.

The Gospel of John

The Gospel of Mark can be the most helpful for those who suffer. But it can also have a deadly impact when victims of abuse, instead of working to end the oppressive situation, suffer in silence, thinking they are following Jesus' example. A different approach is taken by Jesus in the Gospel of John.[5] When one of the policemen strikes Jesus during the interrogation by the high priest, Jesus does not simply take it in silence but retorts, "If I have spoken wrongly, testify to the wrong. But if I have spoken rightly, why do you strike me?" (John 18:23). We turn now to examine some of the ways that the Fourth Evangelist presents the death of Jesus.

Jesus' Death as Birthing New Life

The Fourth Evangelist tells the story of Jesus' life and death in a different key from the other gospel writers.[6] There are a number of metaphors for Jesus' passion and resurrection found in the Gospel of John: the uplifting of the bronze serpent (3:15-16), the giving of his flesh for the life

5. The author of the Fourth Gospel is not known. Our oldest tradition is that it is John, the son of Zebedee, but most biblical scholars today recognize that it is highly unlikely that this disciple, a fisherman from Galilee, would have sufficient education to write such an eloquent text. Moreover, this Gospel likely dates to the 90s, making the son of Zebedee well over a hundred years old. Most people in the first century did not live past forty. In addition, there are clear indications that there was more than one person who had a hand in the final version of the Gospel. Most scholars hold that the Fourth Evangelist was part of the community of the Beloved Disciple, which was likely located near Ephesus. Beyond that, we do not know who he or she was.

6. Much of this material is taken from my essay "Birthed from the Side of Jesus (John 19:34)," in *Finding a Woman's Place: Essays in Honor of Carolyn Osiek*, ed. David L. Balch and Jason T. Lamoreaux, PTMS (Eugene, OR: Pickwick Publications, 2011), 191-211, and chapter 5 of my book *Taking Up the Cross*.

of the world (6:51), the outpouring of water at the Feast of Tabernacles (7:38–39), a good shepherd who lays down his life for his sheep (10:11), seed that must die before it can bring forth fruit (12:24), and washing of feet as a model for serving friends in love to the death (13:1–20). One other image, which we will explore now in detail, is Jesus' death as the birthing of new life.

There is a detail in the Johannine crucifixion scene not found in the other gospels. Just after Jesus dies, "one of the soldiers pierced his side with a spear, and at once blood and water came out" (19:34). Much has been written about the symbolism of the blood and water, but one meaning is that, just as blood and water are the two liquids that accompany the birth process, so the death of Jesus is to be understood as the birthing of the renewed people of God. The evangelist has woven the theme of birthing throughout the whole gospel, and here it reaches its climax.

Born of God From the very opening lines of the Prologue, there is language about birthing. John 1:3 tells us that, through the Word, "all things came into being, not one thing came into being except through him." What is not entirely evident in most English translations is that the verb *ginomai,* usually translated "came into being," has a more specific meaning: "to be born." John 1:3 could be rendered "all things *were birthed* through him." A few verses later, the Prologue speaks about how we become children of God through belief in the Word: "But to all who received him, who believed in his name, he gave power to become *(genesthai)* children of God, who were born *(egennēthēsan)* not of blood or of the will of the flesh or of the will of man, but of God" (1:12–13). In addition to the verb *ginomai* (v. 3), "to become, to be born," John also uses the verb *gennaō* in vv. 12-13, which means "to give birth" and usually refers to female birthing (e.g., John 3:4; 16:21) rather than male begetting.[7] John 1:13 emphasizes that the birthing of God's children comes about through divine action and contrasts with human procreation, which originates in human desire ("will of the flesh")—more precisely, that of males ("the will of man"). "Not of blood" likely refers to the belief in antiquity that conception occurred through the mingling of woman's blood with male seed. The Prologue sets the stage for an understanding of discipleship that entails acceptance of one's birth as a child of God and empowerment to engender life in others through faith in the Word.

---

7. It is used in the sense of male begetting in 8:41; 9:34.

The Birthing of Jesus' Public Ministry The symbol of the waters of birth, introduced in the Prologue, is carried forward in the second chapter, in the scene of the wedding feast at Cana. It is here that Jesus' public ministry is born, and where, for the first time, the disciples are said to believe in him. Jesus' mother is the one who initiates the process.

> ¹On the third day there was a wedding in Cana of Galilee, and the mother of Jesus was there. ²Jesus and his disciples had also been invited to the wedding. ³When the wine gave out, the mother of Jesus said to him, "They have no wine." ⁴And Jesus said to her, "Woman, what concern is that to you and to me? My hour has not yet come." ⁵His mother said to the servants, "Do whatever he tells you." ⁶Now standing there were six stone water jars for the Jewish rites of purification, each holding twenty or thirty gallons. ⁷Jesus said to them, "Fill the jars with water." And they filled them up to the brim. ⁸He said to them, "Now draw some out, and take it to the chief steward." So they took it. ⁹When the steward tasted the water that had become wine, and did not know where it came from (though the servants who had drawn the water knew), the steward called the bridegroom ¹⁰and said to him, "Everyone serves the good wine first, and then the inferior wine after the guests have become drunk. But you have kept the good wine until now." ¹¹Jesus did this, the first of his signs, in Cana of Galilee, and revealed his glory; and his disciples believed in him. (John 2:1–11)

It is significant that the mother of Jesus, the one who gave him physical birth, is the one who recognizes "the hour" for the birthing of his public ministry (2:3). Jesus, however, initially responds, "My hour has not yet come" (2:4). Throughout the Fourth Gospel, the "hour" refers to the hour of Jesus' return to the Father, accomplished through his passion, death, resurrection, ascension, and glorification. These are not separate moments, as Luke portrays them, with forty days between the resurrection and ascension and another ten days before the giving of the Spirit at Pentecost. In the Fourth Gospel, this is all one moment, accomplished instantaneously. At two other places, the evangelist affirms "his hour had not yet come" (7:30; 8:20) to explain why Jesus' opponents were not able to arrest him. Not until 12:23 does Jesus announce "the hour has come for the Son of Man to be glorified," and the Last Supper scene opens with "Jesus knew that his hour had come to depart from this world and go to the Father" (13:1). In the farewell discourse to his disciples, Jesus interprets his "hour" in terms of birthing. He likens his coming passion to the pains of a woman in labor and assures his followers of the ensuing joy at the new birth (16:20-22).

The Cana scene is intimately tied to the crucifixion of Jesus by the figure of Jesus' mother. In both scenes Jesus addresses her as *gynai,* "woman" (2:4; 19:26), and both make reference to "the hour" (2:4; 19:27) and to belief (2:11; 19:35). The symbol of water also links the two. In the Cana episode, the one who gave Jesus physical birth draws him forth and assists in the birth of his public mission, as would a midwife in the birth of a child. In the crucifixion scene, she witnesses the completion of his earthly life and ministry and is midwife to the birth of the renewed community of disciples, who will carry on the next phase of his mission.

Born from Above in Water and the Spirit Between the Cana scene and the crucifixion, other episodes build on the symbolism of water and blood and rebirth. In chapter 3 Jesus engages in a lengthy conversation with Nicodemus about the necessity of being "born again" or "born from above" (there is a word play here involving two meanings of the Greek word *anōthen*) in order to see the kingdom of God (3:3). Nicodemus takes Jesus literally and cannot comprehend how one can be "born again." Jesus explains that being "born from above" means birth in water and the Spirit. It is in the crucifixion scene that the meaning of birth in water and the Spirit comes clear. At Jesus' death, he hands over the Spirit (19:30), as water flows from his pierced side (v. 34). The symbols of water and Spirit signal a rebirth accomplished by divine action, just as Ezekiel prophesied, "I will sprinkle clean water upon you . . . and a new spirit I will put within you" (Ezek 36:25-27).

Life-Giving Water The encounter of Jesus with the Samaritan woman also advances the theme of birthing through the symbols of water and spirit. Jesus offers her "living water" (4:10) that will become "a spring of water gushing up to eternal life" (v. 14). The meaning of "living water" is further developed in the scene during the Feast of Dedication, where Jesus cries out, "Let anyone who is thirsty come to me, and let the one who believes in me drink. As the Scripture has said, 'Out of the believer's heart [*koilia*] shall flow rivers of living water.' Now he said this about the Spirit, which believers in him were to receive; for as yet there was no Spirit, because Jesus was not yet glorified" (7:37-39). In v. 38 the word *koilia,* often translated in this passage as "heart,"[8] is actually the word for "womb, uterus," as in John 3:4,

8. It is also translated "from within" (NAB) or "out of his belly" (KJV).

where Nicodemus asks, "Can one enter a second time into the mother's womb [*koilia*] and be born?" The water flowing from the womb of Jesus in 7:37-39 points ahead to the water that flows from his pierced side in 19:34.

It is not clear from the Greek text whether "his," the possessive pronoun in 7:38 refers to Jesus or to the believer. When read in light of 19:34, both referents can be understood to be in view. The life-giving mission birthed by Jesus is carried forward by believers, who are not simply receptacles for living water but are themselves channels of it.[9]

Labor Pains in Birthing a Renewed People of God In his final words to his disciples at the Last Supper, Jesus explains to them that they are to understand his passion like the labor pains of a mother giving birth to new life: "When a woman is in labor, she has pain, because her hour has come. But when her child is born, she no longer remembers the anguish because of the joy of having brought a human being into the world. So you have pain now, but I will see you again, and your hearts will rejoice, and no one will take your joy from you" (16:21-22). This same metaphor is also found in the Old Testament for the divine anguish in bringing forth the renewed Israel. Isaiah voices God's struggle to rebirth Israel after the exile, "For a long time I have held my peace, I have kept still and restrained myself; now I will cry out like a woman in labor, I will gasp and pant" (Isa 42:14).[10]

There are also places in the Old Testament where God is portrayed as a midwife, as in Isaiah 66:9, "Shall I open the womb and not deliver? says the LORD; shall I, the one who delivers, shut the womb? says your God."[11] It is interesting to note that these images of birthing occur in texts that speak of two of the most painful times in Israel's history: their enslavement in Egypt and the exile in Babylon. The Fourth Evangelist employs this same metaphor so that the crucifixion of Jesus can be understood as a similar experience of death that God will use to open the way for new life.

Birthed from the Side of Jesus (John 19:34) The evangelist has carefully woven the theme of birthing throughout the Gospel to help us understand the image of the blood and water that come out of Jesus' pierced side at his

9. Stephen D. Moore, "Are There Impurities in the Living Water That the Johannine Jesus Dispenses?," in *A Feminist Companion to John,* vol. 1, ed. Amy-Jill Levine, with Marianne Blickenstaff, FCNT 4 (New York: Sheffield Academic Press, 2003), 87.

10. See also Isa 26:17-19; 49:15; 66:7-8, 12-13. Other places where God is portrayed as a birthing mother include Deut 32:18, Job 38:28-29, and Ps 2:7.

11. See also Ps 22:9-10.

death. The "power to become children of God" that was assured in the Prologue (1:12) is accomplished. The mother of Jesus, who gave him physical birth and who mediated the birth of his public ministry (2:1-11), is present again (19:25). She, along with the Beloved Disciple, Mary Magdalene, his mother's sister, and Mary, the wife of Clopas,[12] witness the fulfillment of Jesus' earthly life and mission and act as midwives in the rebirth of the people who will continue his mission. Nicodemus, who struggled to understand what "born again/from above" could mean (3:1-21), returns with Joseph of Arimathea with about a hundred pounds of myrrh and aloes with which to embalm Jesus' body (19:39). As they wrap Jesus' body with the spices in linen cloths (19:40), images of death and birth meld. They swaddle him with bands of cloth, as with a newborn (Luke 2:7).[13] Jesus' words to Nicodemus about being born by water and the Spirit (3:5) are now accomplished. Jesus' offer of "living water" to the woman of Samaria (4:10) and his promise that from his womb and that of the believer would flow "rivers of living water" (7:38) are brought to fulfillment as he hands over the Spirit (19:30). Jesus' last word, "It is finished" (19:30), is like the declaration of a mother who cries out in joy when the birth pangs are over and her child is born.[14] One additional birthing image occurs in the scene where the risen Christ appears to the disciples in the upper room, breathes on them, and says, "Receive the Holy Spirit" (20:22). He breathes the breath of life into the rebirthed community just as a midwife blows breath into the nostrils of a newborn to help it breathe on its own, and just as the Creator did with the first human being, so that it became a "living being" (Gen 2:7). Similarly, Ezekiel prophesied the rebirth of Israel, proclaiming over the valley of dry bones, "I will cause breath to enter you, and you shall live" (Ezek 37:5).

A Long History of Interpreting Jesus' Death as Birth

Long before the birth of modern methods of feminist biblical interpretation, commentators have seen Jesus' passion as labor pangs through which new life is birthed.[15] As early as the turn of the third century, Clement of

---

12. Because there was no punctuation in the original Greek text, it is not clear in 19:25 how many women are standing near the cross.

13. Kitzberger, "Transcending Gender Boundaries in John," 204.

14. Josephine Massyngbaerde Ford, *Redeemer, Friend, and Mother: Salvation in Antiquity and in the Gospel of John* (Minneapolis: Fortress Press, 1997), 196.

15. See further Massyngbaerde Ford, *Redeemer, Friend, and Mother,* 196-97.

Alexandria (153-217) wrote about "the body of Christ, which nourishes by the Word the young brood, which the Lord Himself brought forth in throes of flesh, which the Lord Himself swathed in his precious blood." He then exclaims, "O amazing birth!" (*The Instructor* 1.6).[16] Similarly, Ambrose (d. 397), bishop of Milan, refers to Christ as the "Virgin who bare us, who fed us with her own milk" (*On Virgins* 1.5).[17] A number of Syriac writers make a comparison between Adam's side, which gave birth to Eve, and the pierced side of Jesus, which gave birth to the church. In the Middle Ages, maternal images of Jesus were most prevalent.[18] Julian of Norwich (mid-fourteenth century), for example, says that Jesus "our savior is our true Mother in whom we are endlessly born and out of whom we shall never come."[19] Meister Eckhart (1260-1328), a German Dominican mystic and scholar, mused, "What does God do all day long?" His answer was, "God lies on a maternity bed giving birth all day long."

An Antidote to Atonement Theology

This image of Jesus' death as rebirth has a number of positive aspects. First, it opens a way for female disciples to more readily identify with Christ. The Fourth Evangelist blurs gender boundaries, not only at the crucifixion, but also when speaking of the Logos (grammatically masculine) as birthing all things (1:3), and of the Father having Jesus at his breast, like a nursing mother (1:18).[20] This same image is replicated at the Last Supper, where the Beloved Disciple, who can be any one of us, is lying on Jesus' breast (13:23), enjoying the same intimacy with him as Jesus does with the Father. This symbolism makes it possible for female

16. For an English translation of the text, see www.ccel.org/ccel/schaff/anf02.vi.iii.i.vi.html.

17. For the English translation of the text, see www.ccel.org/ccel/schaff/npnf210.

18. See Caroline Walker Bynum, *Jesus as Mother: Studies in the Spirituality of the High Middle Ages* (Berkeley: University of California Press, 1982).

19. Julian of Norwich, *Showings* (New York: Paulist Press, 1978), 292.

20. Many English translations make it difficult to see this image. The phrase *eis ton kolpon tou patros,* "at the bosom of the Father," in 1:18 has a prepositional phrase very similar to the one in 13:23: *en tō kolpō tou Iēsou,* "on the bosom of Jesus." The NRSV and NJB render 1:18 "close to the Father's heart," and 13:23 as "reclining next to" Jesus. The NAB has "who is at the Father's side" (1:18) and "reclining at Jesus' side" (13:23). The Greek noun *kolpos* literally means "bosom, breast." The KJV and NASB render it more accurately as "in the bosom of the Father" (1:18) and "leaning" or "reclining" "on Jesus' bosom" (13:23).

disciples as well as male to know themselves as an icon of the Christ and an image of God.

Another advantage to the birthing imagery found in the Fourth Gospel is that it speaks of Jesus' death as motivated by a love that is mutual and self-replicating, rather than caused by sin that needs to be atoned for. The love it bespeaks is freely received and freely given, resulting in the full flourishing of all life. Finally, with the birthing metaphor, suffering is not seen as deserved or desirable, but as a valuable part of a natural process. It is the consequence of a choice to entrust oneself to love. This metaphor enables us to understand Jesus' self-gift as similar to that of lovers who choose to make painful sacrifices out of love for the other. The ability to endure the suffering comes from the strength of love and from the joy in the new life that results.

As with all theological interpretations, however, there are also pitfalls to the birthing imagery. For one thing, birthing and motherhood can easily be romanticized, overlooking the fact that not all children are conceived in love. Moreover, not all birth pangs give way to joy, as in the case of stillbirth or the birth of an unwanted child or the death of the mother in childbirth.[21]

Mother Jesus and the Mother of Jesus

One other aspect of the birthing theme in the Fourth Gospel that offers liberative possibilities for women is the image of Jesus' mother in the two critical scenes in which she appears: the wedding at Cana (2:1-11) and at the foot of the cross (19:25-27). These scenes are like bookmarks, framing the whole Gospel, and help us to interpret it through the actions of Jesus' mother, the midwife. At Cana, she is not resigned and accepting of the plight in which the hosts and guests find themselves. She takes initiative toward resolving the problem and insists that her son act. Despite his protest, she recognizes it is the correct time for the birthing of his public ministry and does not back down. On a human level, a lack of wine at a wedding is not exactly a situation of injustice that needs to be confronted. But on a theological level, the necessity for Jesus to manifest

21. See further Kathleen Rushton, "The (Pro)creative Parables of Labour and Childbirth (John 3:1-10 and 16:21-22)," in *The Lost Coin: Parables of Women, Work, and Wisdom,* ed. Mary Ann Beavis, The Biblical Seminar 86 (Sheffield: Sheffield Academic Press, 2002), 206-29.

himself so as to begin the birthing process of bringing disciples to belief in him was a matter of life and death. Jesus' mother is a model of perceptiveness and persistence, encouraging us to enlist the help of others when we recognize the opportune moments to initiate change that will bring about new life.

The image of Jesus' mother standing near the cross is traditionally seen as a sorrowful mother who is helpless to stop her son's execution, and who can only offer her pain up to God. Another way to view her is as a witness to the injustice of Jesus' execution, who protests it by her presence and her testimony. She refuses to let the death-dealing empire have the upper hand, as she once again mediates the birth of new life, acquiring new children in the community of the Beloved Disciple and nurturing their mission, as she first did with her biological son. In the Fourth Gospel, Jesus' mother, like the Beloved Disciple, is never named, allowing us to see ourselves in her place as mothers and midwives of a new creation.

FOR DISCUSSION

1. How do you understand "taking up the cross" in your journey of discipleship? What "crosses" should not be borne?
2. How is it paradoxically necessary to love oneself in order to deny oneself in the authentic gospel sense?
3. How do the images of Jesus and his mother in the Fourth Gospel speak to you of birthing new life?

FOR FURTHER READING

Brock, Rita Nakashima, and Rebecca Ann Parker. *Provers of Ashes: Violence, Redemptive Suffering, and the Search for What Saves Us.* Boston: Beacon, 2001.

Dewey, Joanna. "'Let Them Renounce Themselves and Take Up Their Cross': A Feminist Reading of Mark 8.34 in Mark's Social and Narrative World." Pages 23–36 in *A Feminist Companion to Mark.* Edited by Amy-Jill Levine, with Marianne Blickenstaff. FCNT 2. Sheffield: Sheffield Academic Press, 2001.

Finlan, Stephen. *Problems with Atonement: The Origins of, and Controversy about, the Atonement Doctrine.* Collegeville, MN: Liturgical Press, 2005.

Gebara, Ivone. *Out of the Depths: Women's Experience of Evil and Salvation.* Translated by Ann Patrick Ware. Minneapolis: Fortress Press, 2002.

Reid, Barbara E. *Taking Up the Cross: New Testament Interpretations through Latina and Feminist Eyes.* Minneapolis: Fortress Press, 2007. Spanish translation: *Reconsiderar la cruz.* Estella, Navarra, Spain: Editorial Verbo Divino, 2009.

Conclusion

As you have responded to the invitation to join Wisdom's feast, to learn the ways of Woman Wisdom as employed in feminist methods of biblical interpretation, there may have been some courses in the banquet that have startled you in a pleasant way. Others may have been distasteful at first but could become an acquired taste. My hope has been to open up new possibilities for the flourishing of all—women, men, and all creation—through analyzing the detrimental effects of some traditional biblical interpretations and exploring new directions by reading with the mind, eyes, and heart of a woman. Sometimes studying the historical and cultural context provides a new understanding. In other instances, attending to the literary context, structure, patterns, rhetorical style, and alternative meanings of words and phrases opens up fresh interpretations. New possibilities emerge by recognizing the biases of the original biblical authors and the diverse theologies represented in the collection of books that make up the Bible. Learning to question assumptions, to read between the lines, to recover the lost stories of women, and to reconstruct the rest of the story is a real art that one can refine with practice.

We have noted some of the women forerunners who have sat at Wisdom's table before us, and we have shared our recipes for liberative methods. We have explored some of the most problematic and some of the most liberative texts in the Scriptures, with an eye toward how fulfilling fare can be provided through them for all. While some may feel sated at the end of this book, my hope is that it will simply serve as an appetizer to entice you to dine more fully on the rich array of feminist biblical work that is now available in supersize portions.

Bibliography

Aquino, María Pilar, Daisy L. Machado, and Jeannette Rodríguez, eds. *A Reader in Latina Feminist Theology*. Austin: University of Texas Press, 2002.

Aquino, María Pilar, and María José Rosado-Nunes. *Feminist Intercultural Theology: Latina Explorations for a Just World*. Studies in Latino/a Catholicism. Maryknoll, NY: Orbis Books, 2007.

Athans, Mary Christine. *In Quest of the Jewish Mary: The Mother of Jesus in History, Theology, and Spirituality*. Maryknoll, NY: Orbis Books, 2013.

Balch, David L., and Jason T. Lamoreaux. *Finding a Woman's Place: Essays in Honor of Carolyn Osiek*. PTMS. Eugene, Ore.: Pickwick Publications, 2011.

Beavis, Mary Ann, ed. *The Lost Coin: Parables of Women, Work, and Wisdom*. Biblical Seminar 86. Sheffield: Sheffield Academic Press, 2002.

Bird, Phyllis. *Missing Persons and Mistaken Identities: Women and Gender in Ancient Israel*. OBT. Minneapolis: Fortress Press, 1997.

Brenner, Athalya, and Carole Fontaine, eds. *A Feminist Companion to Reading the Bible: Approaches, Methods, and Strategies*. Sheffield: Sheffield Academic Press, 1997.

Brock, Ann Graham. *Mary Magdalene, the First Apostle: The Struggle for Authority*. Cambridge, MA: Harvard University Press, 2003.

Brooten, Bernadette. *Women Leaders in the Ancient Synagogue: Inscriptional Evidence and Background Issues*. BJS 36. Chico, Calif.: Scholars Press, 1982.

Brown, Raymond E. *Mary in the New Testament: A Collaborative Assessment by Protestant and Roman Catholic Scholars*. Philadelphia: Fortress Press, 1978.

Bynum, Caroline Walker. *Jesus as Mother: Studies in the Spirituality of the High Middle Ages.* Berkeley: University of California Press, 1982.

Campbell, Joan C. *Phoebe: Patron and Emissary.* Paul's Social Network. Collegeville, MN: Liturgical Press, 2009.

Clifford, Anne. *Introducing Feminist Theology.* Maryknoll, NY: Orbis Books, 2001.

Coloe, Mary L., ed. *Creation Is Groaning: Biblical and Theological Perspectives.* Collegeville, MN: Liturgical Press, 2013.

Eaton, Heather. *Introducing Ecofeminist Theologies.* IFT 12. London: T&T Clark, 2005.

Eisen, Ute. *Women Officeholders in Early Christianity: Epigraphical and Literary Studies.* Collegeville, MN: Liturgical Press, 2000.

Ernst, Allie M. *Martha from the Margins: The Authority of Martha in Early Christian Tradition.* SVC 98. Leiden: Brill, 2009.

Eskenazi, Tamara Cohn, and Andrea L. Weiss. *The Torah: A Women's Commentary.* New York: Women of Reform Judaism, 2008.

Gebara, Ivone. *Out of the Depths: Women's Experience of Evil and Salvation.* Translated by Ann Patrick Ware. Minneapolis: Fortress Press, 2002.

Getty Sullivan, Mary Ann. *Women in the New Testament.* Collegeville, MN: Liturgical Press, 2001.

Grey, Mary C. *Introducing Feminist Images of God.* IFT 7. Cleveland: Pilgrim Press, 2001.

Hearon, Holly E. *The Mary Magdalene Tradition: Witness and Counter-Witness in Early Christian Communities.* Collegeville, MN: Liturgical Press, 2004.

Hearon, Holly E., ed. *Distant Voices Drawing Near: Essays in Honor of Antoinette Clark Wire.* Collegeville, MN: Liturgical Press, 2004.

Isasi-Díaz, Ada María. *Mujerista Theology: A Theology for the Twenty-First Century.* Maryknoll, NY: Orbis Books, 1996.

Johnson, Elizabeth A. *She Who Is: The Mystery of God in Feminist Discourse.* New York: Crossroad Publishing, 1992.

———. *Truly Our Sister: A Theology of Mary in the Communion of Saints.* New York: Continuum, 2003.

———. *Dangerous Memories: A Mosaic of Mary in Scripture; Drawn from "Truly Our Sister."* New York: Continuum, 2004.

Kanyoro, Musimbi R. A. *Introduction to Feminist Cultural Hermeneutics: An African Perspective.* IFT 9. Cleveland: Pilgrim Press, 2002.

Keller, Marie Noël. *Priscilla and Aquila: Paul's Coworkers in Christ Jesus.* Paul's Social Network. Collegeville, MN: Liturgical Press, 2010.

Kwok, Pui-lan. *Introducing Asian Feminist Theology*. IFT 4. Cleveland: Pilgrim Press, 2000.

Levine, Amy-Jill, ed., with Marianne Blickenstaff. *A Feminist Companion to Matthew*. FCNT 1. Sheffield: Sheffield Academic Press, 2001.

———. *A Feminist Companion to Mark*. FCNT 2. Sheffield: Sheffield Academic Press, 2001.

———. *A Feminist Companion to Luke*. FCNT 3. Sheffield: Sheffield Academic Press, 2002.

———. *A Feminist Companion to John*. 2 vols. FCNT 4–5. Cleveland: Pilgrim, 2003.

———. *A Feminist Companion to Paul*. FCNT 6. Cleveland: Pilgrim, 2004.

———. *A Feminist Companion to the Deutero-Pauline Epistles*. FCNT 7. London: T&T Clark, 2003.

———. *A Feminist Companion to the Acts of the Apostles*. FCNT 9. New York: T&T Clark, 2004.

Levine, Amy-Jill, ed., with Maria Mayo Robbins. *A Feminist Companion to the Catholic Epistles and Hebrews*. FCNT 8. London: T&T Clark, 2004.

———. *A Feminist Companion to Mariology*. FCNT 10. London: T&T Clark, 2005.

Madigan, Kevin, and Carolyn Osiek. *Ordained Women in the Early Church: A Documentary History*. Baltimore: Johns Hopkins University Press, 2005.

Massyngbaerde Ford, Josephine. *Redeemer, Friend, and Mother: Salvation in Antiquity and in the Gospel of John*. Minneapolis: Fortress Press, 1997.

McFague, Sallie. *Models of God: Theology for an Ecological, Nuclear Age*. Philadelphia: Fortress Press, 1987.

Mitchem, Stephanie Y. *Introducing Womanist Theology*. Maryknoll, NY: Orbis Books, 2002.

Moltmann-Wendel, Elisabeth. *The Women around Jesus*. New York: Crossroad Publishing, 1987.

Moody, Linda A. *Women Encounter God: Theology across the Boundaries of Difference*. Maryknoll, NY: Orbis Books, 1996.

Newsom, Carol A., Sharon H. Ringe, and Jacqueline E. Lapsley, eds. *Women's Bible Commentary*. 3d rev. ed. Louisville: Westminster John Knox, 2012.

Nowell, Irene. *Women in the Old Testament*. Collegeville, MN: Liturgical Press, 1997.

Osiek, Carolyn. *Beyond Anger: On Being a Feminist in the Church*. New York: Paulist Press, 1986.

Osiek, Carolyn, and Margaret Y. MacDonald, with Janet H. Tulloch. *A Woman's Place: House Churches in Earliest Christianity*. Minneapolis: Fortress Press, 2006.

Pomeroy, Sarah B. *Goddesses, Whores, Wives, and Slaves: Women in Classical Antiquity*. New York: Dorset, 1975.

Praeder, Susan Marie. *The Word in Women's Worlds: Four Parables*. Zacchaeus Studies, New Testament. Wilmington: Glazier, 1988.

Ramshaw, Gail. *God beyond Gender: Feminist Christian God-Language*. Minneapolis: Fortress Press, 1995.

Reid, Barbara E. *Choosing the Better Part? Women in the Gospel of Luke*. Collegeville, MN: Liturgical Press, 1996.

———. *Parables for Preachers*. Vol. 1: *Year A—the Gospel of Matthew;* vol. 2: *Year B—the Gospel of Mark;* vol. 3: *Year C—the Gospel of Luke*. Collegeville, MN: Liturgical Press, 1999–2001. Spanish translation: *Las parábolas: Predicándolas y viviéndolas; Ciclo A, B*. Collegeville, MN: Liturgical Press, 2007–8.

———. *Taking Up the Cross: New Testament Interpretations through Latina and Feminist Eyes*. Minneapolis: Fortress Press, 2007. Spanish translation: *Reconsiderar la cruz: Interpretación latinoamericana y feminista del Nuevo Testamento*. Estella, Navarra, Spain: Editorial Verbo Divino, 2009.

Ruether, Rosemary Radford. *Sexism and God-Talk: Toward a Feminist Theology*. Boston: Beacon, 1983.

———. *Women and Redemption: A Theological History*. Minneapolis: Fortress Press, 1998.

Russell, Letty M., and J. Shannon Clarkson, eds. *Dictionary of Feminist Theologies*. Louisville: Westminster John Knox, 1996.

Schaberg, Jane. *The Illegitimacy of Jesus: A Feminist Theological Interpretation of the Infancy Narratives*. San Francisco: Harper & Row, 1987.

———. *The Resurrection of Mary Magdalene: Legends, Apocrypha, and the Christian Tradition*. New York: Continuum, 2002.

Schneiders, Sandra M. *Written That You May Believe: Encountering Jesus in the Fourth Gospel*. Rev. and exp. ed. New York: Crossroad Publishing, 2003.

Scholz, Susanne. *Introducing the Women's Hebrew Bible*. IFT 13. London: T&T Clark, 2007.

Schottroff, Luise. *Lydia's Impatient Sisters: A Feminist Social History of Early Christianity*. Translated by Barbara Rumscheidt and Martin Rumscheidt. Louisville: Westminster John Knox, 1995.

Schottroff, Luise, and Marie-Teres Wacker, eds. *Feminist Biblical Interpretation: A Compendium of Critical Commentary on the Books of the Bible and Related Literature*. Grand Rapids: Eerdmans, 2012.

Schüssler Fiorenza, Elisabeth. *In Memory of Her: A Feminist Theological Reconstruction of Christian Origins*. New York: Crossroad Publishing, 1984.

———. *Wisdom Ways: Introducing Feminist Biblical Interpretation*. Maryknoll, NY: Orbis Books, 2001.

Schüssler Fiorenza, Elisabeth, ed. *Searching the Scriptures*. 2 vols. New York: Crossroad Publishing, 1993–94.

Seim, Turid Karlsen. *The Double Message: Patterns of Gender in Luke-Acts*. Nashville: Abingdon Press, 1994.

Thurston, Bonnie. *Women in the New Testament: Questions and Commentary*. CNT. New York: Crossroad Publishing, 1998.

Trible, Phyllis. *God and the Rhetoric of Sexuality*. OBT. Philadelphia: Fortress Press, 1978.

———. *Texts of Terror: Literary-Feminist Readings of Biblical Narratives*. Philadelphia: Fortress Press, 1984.

Wainwright, Elaine M. *Women Healing/Healing Women: The Genderization of Healing in Early Christianity*. London: Equinox, 2006.

Walker, Alice. *In Search of Our Mothers' Gardens: Womanist Prose*. New York: Harcourt Brace Jovanovich, 1967, 1983.

Yee, Gale A. *Poor Banished Children of Eve: Woman as Evil in the Hebrew Bible*. Minneapolis: Fortress Press, 2003.

Zagano, Phyllis. *Holy Saturday: An Argument for the Restoration of the Female Diaconate in the Catholic Church*. New York: Crossroad Publishing, 2000.

Subject and Name Index

Scripture Index